AF443756

Caught in the Act

Caught in the Act

THE TRUE ADVENTURES OF A DIVORCE DETECTIVE

by William W. Pearce
with William Hoffer

STEIN AND DAY/*Publishers*/New York

First published in 1976
Copyright © 1976 by William W. Pearce and William Hoffer
All rights reserved
Designed by Ed Kaplin
Printed in the United States of America
Stein and Day/*Publishers*/Scarborough House,
Briarcliff Manor, N.Y. 10510

Library of Congress Cataloging in Publication Data
Pearce, William W.
    Caught in the act.
    1. Adultery—United States. 2. Divorce—United
States. 3. Detectives—United States—Correspond-
ence, reminiscences, etc. I. Hoffer, William,
joint author. II. Title.
HQ806.P4   364.1'53   75-34488
ISBN 0-8128-1891-1

To Shirley Pearce,
whose act I caught fifteen years ago

This book is based on facts. But the names of all the people have been changed, except for those of my wife, Shirley, and five of my assistants: Linda Goodwin, Guy Morgan, Jack Fogerty, Jim Metz, and Jim Trexler. In addition, many of the locations and identifiable details have been disguised. If any of the pseudonyms and details resemble names of or incidents involving actual persons, it is entirely coincidental.

CONTENTS

INTRODUCTION

"Caught in *what* act?" my neighbor, Billy Manley, asked.

"Sex."

"You mean he actually snoops on people while they are making love?"

"Yep."

"Gee . . . does he need any help?"

Hardly. In the past ten years William Wayne Pearce has gotten the goods on more than five hundred adulterers and adulteresses. His subjects have ranged from poor inner-city residents to the highest of Washington, D.C.'s high society.

This book is the product of those ten years and five hundred investigations. Bill has carefully chosen twenty-two case histories from his files to teach the would-be adulterer or adulteress how to avoid being trapped between the sheets. Step by step he paints a picture of how the private detective works. He shows how a detective actually *proves* adultery without hiding under the bed. The final chapter, "How to Commit Adultery Without Getting Caught," should be required reading for any unhappily married man or woman.

These twenty-two true stories provide unique glimpses into a wide variety of bedrooms. There are one-night stands, and there are affairs that continue for many years. Twosomes, threesomes and more-somes cavort through the pages in a variety of heterosexual and homosexual encounters.

But perhaps the most refreshing aspect of the book is that Bill has chosen to talk about some of his failures as well as his successes. The student of adultery can learn much from the few who have gotten away from one of the best bedroom sleuths in the business.

Adultery investigations comprise about 75 percent of Bill's cases. His work on criminal investigations has carried him throughout the United States and Europe, but passion is his real passion. He claims that divorce investigations are far more interesting than criminal cases.

But, if they are sexier, they are also more dangerous. Crime statistics indicate that more policemen are murdered when responding to domestic squabbles than to any other calls. Thus a .38-caliber Colt Cobra revolver is Bill's constant companion whenever he is conducting a surveillance.

His victims not infrequently plot bloody revenge when he sits on the witness stand calmly testifying about semen stains on their bed sheets, but Bill long ago stopped bothering to report the numerous threats against his life. Today, when another threat is recorded by his answering service or received in the office mail, he merely makes a careful note of it and files it in a secret hiding place known only to a few who are pledged to deliver the records to the police if someone should follow through on his vicious promise.

Bill was born and raised in Youngsville, North Carolina, where his father, William James Pearce, served as chief of police and then was elected mayor. For five years Bill worked as bailiff for the District of Columbia court system. Appalled by the poor quality of testimony given by most private detectives, he decided to try the business himself. Now, after ten years, he is one of the nation's top professionals in divorce and child-custody investigations. He has never lost a case in court.

He maintains offices in Washington, D.C., Alexandria, Virginia, and London, England. He prefers to work from a fourth, hidden office, where he and his assistants can prepare their reports without fear of intrusion.

He also maintains an apartment in Alexandria, but this is another front. He lives with his wife, Shirley, and their four children in an undisclosed location outside Washington, D.C.

This book is not intended to be a legal text. Rather, it is an attempt to pass on inside information to the potential victim of America's tangled divorce laws—information that lawyers rarely provide. To be sure, few attorneys will appreciate the effort. While Bill has a high admiration for a handful of divorce attorneys, he holds the great majority of lawyers in contempt.

Partly as a protest against money-grubbing divorce lawyers, he recently opened Divorce & Separation Counselors, Inc., in Alexandria, Virginia. For a fee that is ridiculously modest compared to that of most law firms, the confused spouse can discuss all the options of divorce and separation without committing himself or herself to a course of action.

"So many people feel obligated to proceed with a divorce if they pay the large retainer an attorney usually demands," Bill claims. "I'm convinced that many cases could have been reconciled had they received professional guidance at a modest price."

This book would have been impossible without the cooperation of numerous persons. Most of all we owe our wives, Shirley Pearce and Edie Hoffer, a debt of gratitude for their suggestions and encouragement as well as their patience with long hours of interviewing and writing.

We gratefully acknowledge the professional investigatory work of Bill's assistants, Linda Goodwin, Guy Morgan, Jack Fogerty, Jim Metz, and Jim Trexler.

For legal advice we thank John McCollum, attorney-at-law of Springfield, Virginia.

Finally, a special thank-you to scores of confidential informants who have provided invaluable information but must remain unrecognized. They know who they are.

—WILLIAM HOFFER

1

THE NUMBER-ONE CRIME

The number-one crime in America is not armed robbery, murder, rape, income-tax evasion or running for political office.

It is adultery.

In ten years of work as a private detective I have personally investigated more than five hundred cases of adultery, and I've learned that the mere fact that a person says, "I do!" doesn't seem to stop him from doing it with other partners too. I would estimate that at least half of the "happily married" couples in America cheat.

And if a married couple decide to separate, adultery is a virtually certain by-product. Before granting a divorce decree most states demand a waiting period far longer than the average sexual appetite can endure. In my experience, nearly every man commits adultery within a few weeks of separation from his wife. The wives are sometimes a bit slower to act, but most—perhaps 80 percent—eventually find themselves between the sheets with a new lover.

That's not a crime, you say, that's nature. Maybe so, but the pious legislators of our state and local governments have declared otherwise. In most localities in the United States adultery is a misdemeanor, punishable by a fine or jail or both. To be sure, very few adulterers are ever prosecuted as common criminals, but it does happen. Particularly when a very vindictive spouse has been hurt, the adulterer can be in for a nasty battle with the American judicial system.

Modern society no longer requires a sinner to walk the streets wearing a scarlet letter. In our civilized manner we simply punish the adulterer by removing his money and children. Or her money and children. When a private detective can prove a case of adultery his client can look for a generous divorce settlement. Adultery is a prime consideration in child-custody decisions, too. Today's judges are no longer reluctant to award custody to the father if we can paint a courtroom picture of a sexually depraved mother. And more than one modern judge has even ordered an adulteress to pay alimony and child support to her husband.

The adultery game is played for high stakes, yet it is often played foolishly. I feel that, given enough time and money, I can trap almost any man or woman who is committing adultery. Yet most of my investigations are boringly routine because the lovers make so little attempt at secrecy.

Don't misunderstand me. I'm no prude. I have committed adultery myself. I believe that whatever is done in private by two or more consenting adults is fine. But I will never understand how an otherwise intelligent, rational person can risk everything for a few moments of illicit sex when a few precautions would have saved a lot of embarrassment, trouble and money.

This book is designed to help you avoid the Play Now, Pay Later trap. I'll show you how an adultery detective does his job, and how you can complicate and confound his snooping. Can you tell if you are being followed? Do you know how a detective *proves* adultery without actually witnessing the sex act? Are you aware that you and your illicit lover can commit certain sex acts that are not legally defined as adultery? Do you know the ways that your conversations can be bugged? Do you know how you can destroy a detective's entire case with one big lie?

Whether you are male or female; whether you have a steady lover or like to play the field; whether you are cheating secretly on a spouse or openly swapping; whether you are straight, gay or AC-DC . . . if you are a participant in America's number one criminal activity, you would be wise to study the following twenty-two case histories from my personal files.

Consider the plight of Sidney Miller.

I listened to the groans and sighs of Sid's ecstasy as they blared forth from my tape recorder while I drove to see him recently. But the sounds of his passion were whispers compared to his screams of agony as a trapped adulterer. Once rich, happy and ambitious, his sexual stupidity ruined his marriage and his career. Today even his life is in jeopardy.

Several years ago Sid landed a job with an accounting firm in Washington, D.C., and helped build the business to a prosperous level. He eventually became vice president and—when the company founder retired—president. His office wall was papered with degrees and certificates attesting to his skills as an accountant. He was a director of two of the largest banks in the District and president of a local charity.

This pillar of Washington society made the classic mistake of screwing his secretary. This is among the more stupid forms of adultery because the secretary knows too much about a man's business. She may seem like a sweet and ardent puppy in the beginning, but she has a potential for becoming a large-size bitch. If the boss gives the slightest sign that he is ready to drop the relationship, the secretary will bristle with thinly veiled hints of personal or business blackmail.

Claire, Sid's secretary, was lonely. Her husband, Paul, was doing three to five years in the Maryland state penitentiary for beating his best friend to death during a barroom argument. Paul is one of those poor human animals cursed with an uncontrollable temper.

Claire is not very pretty, but she was accessible and horny. Paul had not been in prison very long before Claire was taking more than dictation from Sid when she remained at the office for evening work. For nearly two years the affair continued without incident.

But the lovers knew that, sooner or later, Paul and his fearsome temper would be released from prison. Claire wrote to tell Paul she wouldn't be "tying any yellow ribbons around the old oak tree." Wisely, she gave no hint that she was involved with another man. For the sake of their four-year-old girl, Claire lied, she did not want Paul to return home.

Paul was hurt and mad, but he had to stay out of trouble or he would violate his parole. Since he did not suspect Claire's adultery, he managed to accept her decision. After his release he rented a house and went into business for himself as a bricklayer. Claire and Sid tried to be extra careful. They did not go out together in public and confined their sexual relations to Sid's office couch.

But Sid's mind was on his affair, not his business. He ignored his management duties, and several employees began to take advantage of him. Three of them seemed particularly lazy, but when Sid finally decided to fire them, they openly hinted that they knew of the adultery.

And there was Paul. Since leaving prison he had uttered threats against the policeman who had arrested him, the district attorney who had prosecuted him, and the judge who sentenced him. He often plagued Claire with telephone calls full of drunken abuse, including his growing suspicion that Claire's sexual desires were well satisfied. Sid had few doubts as to how Paul would react to the man who had seduced his wife.

But, as often happens, Sid's lover had become the most immediate threat. She was beginning to apply the "when are you going to divorce your wife and marry me?" pressure. He had no desire to leave his wife, his children and his $70,000 home.

It was then that a very shaken Sid called me. He hoped to

buy time by getting Claire to divorce Paul. The plan was a good one—Claire would become involved in her own legal battle, and the courts would prevent Paul from harassing her. But, in order to succeed, the divorce had to be granted quickly.

The three hostile employees were becoming bolder in their threats. Divorce on most grounds would require a twelve- to eighteen-month delay. Divorce on the grounds of adultery would be immediate.

I winced as Sid told me the details of the story, but I agreed to help. Paul, said Sid, was a firm believer in the double standard. Though any thought of Claire's adultery would stir a murderous rage within him, he had found a young girlfriend for himself. The circumstances were right for an easy investigation.

Sid paid me a large retainer out of his personal funds. Then he called Claire into the office. Her cheeks flushed as we talked, but she gave me Paul's address, a description of his pickup truck and a photograph of the huge, mean-looking man she had married.

By its nature, of course, adultery is a private crime. The law recognizes that most evidence of it must be circumstantial. A judge will generally uphold the accusation if we can show an adulterous inclination, the opportunity to commit adultery and suspicious circumstances. In our investigations we take highly detailed notes. Trivia about the color of clothing, the brand of cigarettes or the number of drinks consumed has an authentic ring in court. We always employ at least two investigators so that the testimony of one corroborates the other. Generally, we build a web of circumstantial evidence that is devastating.

In this case, however, we were to witness the adultery firsthand.

Our investigation began on a Tuesday. My assistant, Jack Fogerty, and I drove up near Paul's house about four o'clock in the afternoon. Jack is a former state highway patrolman who stands six feet three and weighs about 240. Usually his size is an asset, but twice during this investigation I was to regret his bulk.

The neighborhood was a typical middle-class suburb, and most of the modest homes were well groomed. Paul's house was the eyesore on the block. The grass was over a foot tall, and a window was broken. Throughout the house the venetian blinds were in disarray, twisted and bent.

The house appeared deserted. I knocked on the front door, rather confident that no one would answer. (If someone had come I would have posed as an insurance salesman.) But there was no reply, so we indicated in our notes that the house was empty.

We waited an hour and a half until Paul drove up in his truck. Watching through binoculars from my vantage point down the street, I could see a woman in the truck with him. She was pressed up close to Paul, with her left arm around his shoulders. I wondered if she knew that she was hugging a killer.

They walked into the house hand in hand. Using a telephoto lens, Jack snapped several clear shots of them. The photos would be evidence of public signs of affection—one of the bits of circumstantial evidence pointing to an inclination to commit adultery. Jack and I kept both entrances under surveillance for two hours. Finally the couple left the house and drove off.

We followed our subjects to a restaurant about a mile away and took a table across the room from them. Paul ordered a pitcher of beer—a good sign that they would remain for some time, so Jack waited at the table while I went back outside.

As I had hoped, Paul had left his truck unlocked. I had a key that would probably have opened it, but his carelessness saved me the trouble. I slipped into the driver's seat and looked around. A note on the dashboard seemed to be a map for getting to a home about thirty miles north of Washington.

It indicated that a party was to be held at the address on the following Saturday night. I grabbed the scrap of paper, ran next door to a print shop and had a photocopy made, returned the note to the truck and rejoined Jack in the restaurant.

We followed the subjects back home, and after they entered the house we moved closer on foot to see if we could get a view of the inside. But Paul's German shepherd growled ominously every time we approached, so we were forced to continue our surveillance from our car. (A good watchdog, by the way, is a must for the careful adulterer. I am dedicated to my job but I refuse to become the Ken-L Ration for anybody's pooch.) I made a note to deal with the dog later.

By 12:15 the only light we could spot was the blue-white glow of the television screen in the bedroom. We continued our surveillance all night, and when Paul and the girl left the house hand in hand the next morning, we had the beginnings of a pretty solid circumstantial case of adultery.

Our next task was to discover the name of the co-subject— the girl. We followed them that morning as they drove off in Paul's truck, and watched them kiss goodbye in front of an office building. I joined the girl in the elevator and saw her enter the office of a small trade association.

Jack and I had a late breakfast in a nearby diner. After giving the girl a chance to get settled into her office for the morning, I placed a call to the trade assocation, pretending to be a newspaper reporter. I asked for some industry sales statistics, which she supplied.

"You sure have been helpful," I said to her. "You sound so sweet and nice this morning."

"Thank you."

"What's your name?"

"Suzie Carter."

"Well, Suzie Carter, I just happen to have the evening free tonight. How would you like to have dinner?"

"Oh, that sounds like fun," she said. "Except I'm going steady with another guy."

Jack and I reviewed our notes from the night-long surveillance, then drove home for a bit of sleep.

Saturday afternoon we again set up a stakeout near Paul's house. His truck was parked in the driveway but there was no sign of activity inside. The damned dog roamed about the fenced-in yard.

At eight o'clock Paul and Suzie left the house and drove away. Jack and I followed in my car, and I radioed an all-clear signal to Jim Metz, one of my other assistants. We followed Paul at high speed along the Capitol Beltway to Interstate 270. As we suspected, he was following the map that he had so generously left in his unlocked truck. We watched as he stopped at the address on the map, and the two went inside. Carefully, I eased my car into a spot alongside the curb, only two spaces behind Paul's truck.

We waited.

About 10 P.M. Jim called me on the radio. Having once been a deputy sheriff and K-9 officer, Jim knows how to control animals. The fact that he had a bowlful of ground beef in his hands didn't hurt his chances of making friends with Paul's German shepherd. After devouring the food the dog allowed Jim to pet him and carefully slip a leash onto his collar. Jim trotted him away to some nearby woods and tied him to a tree.

I congratulated him and asked him to wait for us in his car near Paul's house.

Most detective work is tedious and exacting. We do not merely sit outside watching a house. We make exact notes of everything we see. If someone—anyone—appears at the window of the house, we note it. We record the exact time when lights go on and off in various rooms. We note the arrival and departure of anyone. The danger of such routine is that it sometimes lulls you into carelessness. At 2:15 we were quietly continuing our surveillance when the door of the house burst open and Paul and Suzie staggered out. They were laughing and talking loudly, and obviously drunk.

We quickly slipped down in our seats, trying to duck out of sight behind the dashboard. I'm not tiny, but big Jack could hardly breathe as he wedged his bulk down toward the floor of the car.

I peeked up over the dash and watched as the couple walked down the sidewalk toward the truck. Suzie got into the cab, but Paul kept right on walking toward us. I ducked back down. My hand automatically reached for my gun. If the murderer had appeared at my window I would have used my gun for the first time in nine hectic years of snooping.

But his footsteps stopped short. The street became silent. Then I heard the sound of water trickling somewhere nearby. Again I peeked.

Paul was relieving himself on the front bumper of my car.

I slipped back down out of sight and tightened the grip on my gun. Jack looked puzzled, but I didn't risk a whisper.

We waited until we heard the truck motor start and move off down the street, then followed them home.

As Paul dragged Suzie drunkenly off to bed we prepared to gather more evidence. Jim, with man's best friend out of the way, had found a ladder in Paul's garage and laid it underneath the bedroom window. The blinds were half open.

I placed the ladder quietly against the house and climbed up. I could see two naked bodies on the bed, illuminated by the faint light of the moon. I now had visual evidence of intercourse, but I needed a second witness. When Jack started up the ladder it groaned under his bulk, so Jim happily took his place. Jim watched the action so long that I finally had to tug hard at his pants to get him down from the ladder.

The attorney's grin nearly matched Jim's when we presented our report on Monday morning. Later that week

Paul was served with divorce papers. A copy of our report was sent to his attorney, and though Paul left several obscene messages on my telephone recorder, he never succeeded in tracking me down. Within two weeks Claire was granted an uncontested divorce on the grounds of adultery. A few weeks later Paul skipped town, leaving a heart-broken girlfriend, an array of creditors and an angry parole officer.

Normally our case would have been closed—with other couples to follow and other windows to peer into. But I had not counted on the fact that my own client was as careless as my subject.

Sid called me three months later and begged me to come see him.

"My wife has gotten a couple of telephone calls from a woman," he said as soon as I entered his office. "The woman said she had a tape of Claire and me making love."

"How did your wife react?"

"Bill, she's always been a good wife. She told me about the calls right away. She said she never suspected me, and she trusted me. I lied like a thief."

"Who do you think it was?"

Sid told me that his three problem employees—a man and two women—had just quit. He was sure the three of them were working together.

"Could they really have a tape?" I asked.

Sid pulled open his desk drawer and pointed to two tape cassettes. "I usually keep three tapes here for my recorder," he said.

"Sid, this is very important. Before these employees quit did you have sex with Claire here in the office?"

"To be honest, Bill, every night after work! Right here on the couch!"

"What are you going to do if the woman calls again?"

"She can't," Sid replied with a grin. "I had our phone number changed today to a private listing."

I stifled an impulse to leap out of my chair and shake Sid by the lapels. Instead, I shook my head and muttered quietly, "You stupid bastard."

Sid looked confused.

"When you tell your wife you did that, she's really going to be suspicious," I pointed out. "At first she thought you had nothing to hide. Now you've proved that you do."

His face paled. Quickly he wrote me out another large retainer from his checkbook. "Get that tape," he pleaded.

Sid figured that the man was the ringleader among the trio of ex-employees, and would be the one most likely to have the tape. Jack and I placed him under surveillance and traced him to a new accounting firm where he had taken a job. The man knew me from my visits to Sid's office, so I had one of my smooth-talking assistants, Jim Trexler, call him up.

Jim pretended to be on the staff of a large investment company. The firm, he lied, was considering the purchase of Sid's company. Since our subject was a former employee, Jim asked if he could supply a character reference for Sid.

The man grabbed eagerly at the bait. He agreed to meet Jim for dinner at a local restaurant. Jim dressed for the occasion, supplementing his blue suit with a microphone hidden under the lapel. Jack sat outside in my car, taping the conversation, while I used a master key to open the trunk of the suspect's car. I've learned that many people with something to hide feel that an automobile trunk is as safe as a bank vault—so naturally it is the first place we look. I found the tape hidden under a blanket.

Meanwhile, Jack was tuning in on an intriguing story. The suspect was trying to maintain his cool. He wanted to damage Sid's reputation, but he was attempting to do so without appearing obvious. He let Jim pull from him veiled accusations of office hanky-panky. Finally he came to something very surprising. Sid, he said, was a complete phony: the impressive array of diplomas that glorified Sid's office wall came from a certain underground print shop in New York City.

Sid has his tape back, but that's about all he has. Enraged at our theft of the evidence, the three employees called Sid at his office and threatened to make their accusations public. I suspect that Sid has paid dearly for their silence.

Claire is still Sid's secretary, but she spends most of her time nagging him to divorce his wife. She has even threatened to confess the adultery in order to force Sid to act, so the poor man pays most of her bills just to keep her quiet. He neglects his business, and most of his larger accounts have transferred to other firms. His wife is openly suspicious now, and has threatened to divorce him and wipe out what is left of his finances.

And lurking in the background is the specter of Paul, who might someday return to town with his vicious temper to find out that his ex-wife dumped him for her boss.

If you don't think adultery is a crime, think about Sid. He has been sentenced to a lifetime of fear.

2

DEADLY DETAILS

Two days after graduating from high school in Youngsville, North Carolina, I put on my Sunday suit and hopped a bus to Raleigh, where I knocked on the door of the resident agent of the Federal Bureau of Investigation. My eighteen-year-old heart nearly broke when he informed me that a college education was necessary to become an agent.

So, instead of becoming a glamorous G-man, I got a job as a bailiff for the District of Columbia Court of General Sessions, thanks to a mild bit of political pull by a relative. Accustomed to the courtroom scenes on television and in the movies, I was appalled by the shoddy reality of everyday justice. Divorce cases in particular seemed like a lottery, won by whoever happened to obtain the better lawyer. From my seat on the bailiff's bench it seemed that the great majority of divorce cases were presented in a careless, incompetent manner.

The rare attorney who came to divorce court with an ironclad case often had one particular distinguishing characteristic. He was generous—generous enough, that is, to share some of his client's money with a private detective.

At first I had contempt for a man who would spy on human sexual encounters in exchange for a fee. But I soon realized that, like the trashman who collects your garbage, the private detective is a very necessary part of our imperfect world.

Society's laws, it seemed to me, were attempting to place

inhuman constraints on a very human drive. In many states the law forces a married couple to wait one, two—even three—years before their breakup is declared official. Often the only way to get out of the interminable waiting period is to prove adultery against the spouse. Almost without exception the only way for a husband to gain custody of his children is to prove adultery against the wife.

But proving adultery is a difficult task.

After five years of watching others try to document acts of extramarital sex, I could no longer sit on the sidelines. I had my own ideas of how to do the job, and I wanted to try them out. So I got my license as a private investigator.

A private detective collects incriminating evidence one piece at a time until its weight is overwhelming. The best way to illustrate how these details are accumulated is to invite you into the courtroom during my testimony in a recent case. It is not a particularly remarkable case, for it concerns an average housewife who was having an affair with one of her husband's fellow employees. But it provides a textbook case of adultery.

We will pick up the testimony shortly after I have been sworn in on the witness stand. My client is the husband; and I am being questioned by his attorney.

Q. Where did she arrive?

A. At 3:01 P.M. Mrs. Warner arrived at the valet parking entrance at Union Station in Washington, D.C.

Q. Did she park her vehicle?

A. She parked in the valet parking.

Q. What occurred after she parked there?

A. She removed the luggage from the car and placed it on a cart provided by the attendants.

Q. And where did she go?

A. Inside Union Station.

Q. When she arrived at the station, was she alone?

A. Alone. Yes, sir.

Q. What did she do while in the station?

A. At 3:33 P.M Mrs. Warner inquired of a ticket agent the track number for the 5:05 train to New York.

Q. Did you hear this?

A. Yes, I did. I also heard her informed that it was departing from Track 24.

Q. What occurred after this?

A. At 3:50 P.M. Mrs. Warner, whom we had observed pushing her cart inside of the foyer area of Union Station, appeared to be looking for someone.

Q. Did there come a time when she did meet someone?

A. Yes.

Q. When was that?

A. At 4:38 P.M.

Q. Whom did she meet?

A. She met Mr. Harmon.

Q. What was he wearing?

A. He was attired in a brown imitation-suede coat and a turtleneck sweater, blue dungarees, brown socks, tan engineer-type cowboy boots. His hair was much longer that day than it is today.

Q. Is there any question in your mind that the man you saw today was Harmon, the same man?

A. No question of that.

Q. All right. What did they do when they met?

A. At 4:43 P.M. Mrs. Warner and Mr. Harmon were at the Avis Car Rental booth and talking. At 4:45 both Mrs. Warner and Mr. Harmon completed a transaction with one of the ticket agents, the nature of which we could not observe due to the number of persons at the ticket window at the time. They left the ticket window and walked toward Track 24.

Q. What did they do at Track 24?

A. They took the 5:05 train to New York.

Q. Did you have tickets for that train?

A. Yes, sir, we did.

Q. How was it that you had tickets for that train?

A. So that we could make sure that we would be on the

same train, we purchased tickets for all the trains leaving for New York.

Q. What happened when they arrived on the train?

A. At 4:50 P.M. Mrs. Warner and Mr. Harmon entered car 2809. They placed their luggage in the rack above the seat they were in, seat number 44.

Q. What did you next observe between them?

A. I observed Mrs. Warner and Mr. Harmon embrace and they both kissed. This continued all the way to New York, the kissing, the embracing between Mrs. Warner and Mr. Harmon. She was also observed rubbing the inner thigh of Harmon's leg on the train to New York.

Q. Did you see this?

A. Yes, I did.

Q. When did the train arrive, and where?

A. Eight-forty-one P.M. arrived at Penn Station, New York City.

Q. What took place after they arrived at the station?

A. They took a cab and they went to the Hotel Lexington at 48th Street and Lexington Avenue, arriving there at 9:01 P.M.

Q. On arriving at the hotel, what did they do?

A. They both entered the hotel together. Mr. Harmon registered at the desk as Mr. and Mrs. Roger Harmon. While he was registering at the desk, Mrs. Warner was at his side.

Q. Did you observe this registration card?

A. Yes, I did, and I recorded the folio number.

Q. What was the number?

A. AX36784. They were assigned room 2625 for one night, and he paid $36.78 for the room.

Q. How did he pay this money?

A. He paid cash.

Q. Go ahead.

A. Bellman number 19 at the Hotel Lexington, his name is George . . .

Q. Let me stop here for a second, Mr. Pearce, to clarify.

Everything you are testifying to, I want to be sure it is what you personally observed and no one else.

A. That's right. I understand that.

Q. All right. You referred to a bellman. Now, what did he do?

A. The bellman assisted Mrs. Warner and Mr. Harmon to room 2625.

Q. What happened when they arrived at the room?

A. They all entered. The bellman returned to the hall, and both Mrs. Warner and Mr. Harmon were in the room 2625 together.

Q. At what time was that?

A. Nine-oh-five p.m.

Q. Did there come a time that they left the room?

A. Yes, sir.

Q. And when was that?

A. At 10:01 P.M.

Q. Did you observe what they did when they left the room?

A. They took the elevator to the lobby and entered a Yellow cab.

Q. Did you follow them to the lobby?

A. Yes, I did. . . . Matter of fact, I was on the elevator with them when they went to the lobby.

By slipping a bill to the desk clerk, my associate and I managed to rent a room about twenty-five feet down the hall from our subjects. While they were out for the evening we made careful preparations. First we placed a small mirror in the hallway so that, by lying flat on the floor at the door of our room, we could observe the door of room 2625.

Then we taped the door.

The term "tape" derives from an old detective technique. An investigator would appear too conspicuous if he tried to lurk all night in the hallway of a hotel or apartment, yet he has to verify the fact that a couple remained together inside their room. My predecessors developed the technique of sticking a tiny piece of masking tape over the edge of the hotel or apartment door. If they witnessed a couple enter a room, and if the tape remained in place all night, they could testify that the couple had spent the night together.

The technique worked well until a defense attorney, in a dramatic courtroom demonstration, proved that it was possible for the door to open and for the tape to stick once again after the door was shut.

We had to find a new method, so today our "tape" is a matchstick. We simply bend a cardboard match in the middle and shove it into the hinged side of the door, down low where it will be out of sight. If the door is opened the matchstick will drop. Every time. We check the "tape" periodically during the entire period of surveillance. As long as the match remains in place we can confidently testify that the couple remained inside.

Q. Where were you now, after they departed in the cab?

A. We maintained a surveillance in the lobby at the Hotel Lexington. We did not follow Mrs. Warner and Mr. Harmon.

Q. Did they return?

A. Four-thirty-two A.M Mrs. Warner and Mr. Harmon returned to the hotel. They entered the main entrance of the lobby.

Q. Was there any contact between them?

A. No.

Q. What did you next observe about them?

A. Four-thirty-four A.M. Mrs. Warner and Mr. Harmon left the elevator on the twenty-sixth floor and went to room 2625, where they both entered.

Q. What did you do after they entered the room?

A. We taped the door.

Q. What occurred next, in regard to your activities?

A. At 5:30 A.M. we checked the door.

Q. All right.

A. At 6:30 A.M. I checked the door. The tape was still intact. No sounds could be heard coming from the room.

Q. What was the next thing you observed in reference to the activity in the room, or when was the next time the tape was checked?

A. Seven-thirty A.M., and the tape was still intact. We had constant surveillance of the room by means of a mirror we had set up in the hall.

Q. Did you go to sleep?

A. No.

Q. What was the next activity in regards to the room—not your room, the room they were in?

A. At 8:05 A.M. the maid opened the door to 2625 with a passkey, but then she closed it immediately.

Q. What did you observe next?

A. At 8:07 Mr. Harmon opened the door. He was nude from the waist up. He reached out, put the "Do Not Disturb" sign on the door knob and closed the door.

Q. Do you know what he was wearing from the waist down?

A. No.

Q. After he put the "Do Not Disturb" sign on the door, what did you do in reference to the door?

A. It was retaped immediately.

Q. Was there continuous checking of the tapes?

A. Yes, sir. At 8:30 A.M. tape was still intact; no sounds could be heard from the room.

Q. Next time the tape was checked?

A. Nine-thirty A.M., still intact.

Q. Next time?

A. Ten-thirty A.M. Tape still intact.

Q. Did there come a time when you could hear sounds?

A. At 12:02 P.M. I checked the tape, and I did hear talking in the room, but I could not understand the conversation.

Q. Were there further sounds later?

A. Yes, at 12:05.

Q. What did you hear?

A. Noise—there was a bouncing noise like someone jumping on a bed and Mrs. Warner—I will quote exactly what I heard her say—

Q. All right.

A. She said, "Oh, oh, oh, oh." Four times, in a loud voice. Also, "Oh, my God, honey. Oh, honey," and that was it.

Q. When was the next time you heard activity in the room?

A. At 2:05 P.M.

Q. Were you able to hear anything?

A. It sounded as though someone was jumping on a bed, and I can also quote exactly what Mrs. Warner was saying.

Q. What did you hear Mrs. Warner say?

A. She repeated the "Oh, oh, oh, oh . . . ah, ah, ah, ah," and at the same time the noise was continuing to come from the bed.

Q. All right.

A. She also said, "Oh, hon," which could be heard a measured eighteen feet from the subjects' room.

Q. What next did you hear in regard to activity in the room?

A. Two-eighteen P.M., tape was still intact. Shower was running. You could hear from the hallway.

Q. Next activity that you may have heard?

A. At 2:26 P.M. Mr. Harmon asked, "Where in the hell are all the towels?" The shower ceased. Could hear movement in the room, but I could not understand the conversations.

Q. What took place next?

A. Two-forty-four P.M. Mrs. Warner and Mr. Harmon, attired as previously mentioned, left room 2625 with their luggage and proceeded to the elevator.

Q. And did you see them yourself?

A. Yes, I did. I took the elevator with them.

Q. What happened when they arrived in the lobby?

A. Two-fifty P.M., on exiting from the elevator at the lobby they proceeded to the sidewalk in front of the hotel with part of the luggage. Mr. Harmon proceeded to the registration desk, where he handed the clerk a room key and walked toward the main entrance of the hotel to join Mrs. Warner.

Q. And what did you do then?

A. Well, at 2:52 P.M. Mr. Harmon and Mrs Warner entered a New York Yellow cab with the luggage.

Q. Did you follow the cab?

A. No.

Q. What did you do next?

A. At 3:20 P.M. we entered room 2625 and examined the room. We found what appeared to be semen stains on the sheet of the bed. There was an unopened pack of Vantage cigarettes on the nightstand and an empty package in the trash can in the bathroom. There were no other items that we could find in the room.

Such testimony, backed up by an associate investigator, is virtually impossible to refute. And, in this case, Mrs. Warner's own attorney helped strengthen the charges. He sauntered toward me for cross-examination, confident that he could tear down a portion of my testimony:

Q. It says here that there were what appeared to be semen stains on the bed sheet.

A. That's correct.

Q. Did you have any chemical tests made of the stains you found?

A. No, but I'm familiar with what semen stains look like.

Q. How are you familiar with them?

A. Well, I've been married for fourteen years. I know what semen stains are.

Whereupon, the entire courtroom burst into laughter, except for the attorney, Mr. Harmon, and the red-faced Mrs. Warner.

3

THE SMUGGLER AND
THE SECRETARY

"The devil will take care of William," Dorothy Preston snapped.

"Perhaps I can help the devil take care of William," I replied.

Dorothy looked at me carefully. "Perhaps," she acknowledged.

She then related a story that was to put me on the track of her husband—one of the most mysterious gentlemen I have ever followed.

William Preston had worked for the federal government all his life, filling diplomatic posts in Japan, the Ryukyu Islands, Korea and Pakistan. He constantly traveled from those bases, making quick stops in other countries around the globe to handle special, top-secret assignments. He never explained to Dorothy exactly what he did on these trips—they were always referred to as "diplomatic missions." In 1965 he was sent to South Vietnam as a public-safety adviser. By 1970 he was permanently assigned to Washington, but he still traveled a great deal for Uncle Sam.

William may have been a diplomat, but he was not very diplomatic. He often taunted Dorothy with hints that he had met many beautiful young girls on his world travels. Now that his sixty-seven-year-old wife was almost an invalid, suffering from high blood pressure and attacks of nervous tension, William had become more bold in his amorous adventures. Several times he had come home with lipstick on his underwear!

Gently I told Mrs. Preston the things I would need for a proper adultery investigation. I asked to see a photograph of William. The pudgy old man struck me as a most unlikely stud—he was fifty-four, but he could have passed for seventy. A flabby five-foot-eight frame supported his bloated face, squinting eyes, and bulbous nose. Fluffy white hair popped out from either side of his head like a circus clown's. Yet, judging by his employment record, he was obviously a capable man who might well be a sneaky, even dangerous, subject to track into a strange bedroom.

I asked Dorothy if she suspected any woman in particular. She said no, but William frequently reminisced about the seventeen-year-old secretary who worked for him when he was stationed in Karachi. She was the daughter of an American businessman who lived in the Pakistan capital.

"Do you know if he has a photograph of her?" I asked.

She rose wearily and walked over to her husband's desk at one end of the library in their magnificent home in Potomac, Maryland. In a few moments she returned with a crumpled snapshot.

"I found this under some papers," she said.

Though the girl was only seventeen at the time of the photograph, she was well-developed. Long dark hair flowed down below her shoulders, caressing a body that could entice any man. But, despite her natural sexiness, her smile radiated innocence. Could this girl possibly have been sexually involved with pudgy old William?

"Is there anyone else he talks about?" I asked Dorothy. "What about his current secretary?"

"Oh, no," Dorothy assured me. "Diana would never become involved with William, I'm sure. She's such a nice little girl. She calls here all the time."

"What's her last name?"

"Uh . . . Norris, I think."

"What does she look like?"

"I don't know. I've never met her."

The distraught woman could not supply me with any additional leads. But if we could come to terms on a fee, I was ready to begin an investigation. Judging by the appearance of the home, money would be no problem. Thick Persian rugs glowed on the polished hardwood floors, and a fantastic array of Eastern art works dazzled me.

However, when I asked for my usual retainer of $1,000, Dorothy's face dropped.

"I only have $500," she said, holding a wad of bills out to me. "But when I play Bingo Tuesday night I'll win another $300. You may have that, too."

"What?"

"William doesn't give me any money, except a few dollars a week for groceries. I take the grocery money to the firehouse and play Bingo. Tuesday I'll win $300."

Something prompted me not to pursue the conversation, and I agreed to the terms. If I could win a good divorce settlement for Dorothy Preston I knew I'd have no trouble collecting my fee. To raise the money she would only have to sell a few pieces of the fantastic art collection.

So I began, with the remainder of my fee dependent upon Lady Luck.

William drove a car that vaguely resembled himself: a pudgy old pink Plymouth. It was easy to spot in the parking lot of the office building where he worked. Jim Metz and I staked it out late that afternoon. We were in separate cars to make surveillance easier.

About 4:45 we got our first glimpse of the world traveler. He tottered out the front door of the building, made his way to the car, and sat behind the wheel with his eyes closed. Ten minutes later a statuesque girl emerged from the building and walked toward the same car. Long dark hair streamed down over her shoulders. A red mini-dress showed off perfect legs. She walked directly toward William's car, opened the passenger door, and slid over next to the old man.

I pulled a photo out of my pocket and stared at it in disbelief. She had matured in eight years, but it was the same girl William had known in Pakistan!

We followed the car to the Georgetown section of Washington. William was a poky driver who took his time to find a parking space, allowing me the opportunity to park my car in front of a fire hydrant, hop out onto the sidewalk, and pose as a pedestrian. I was about thirty feet behind the couple when they entered the lobby of an old five-story apartment building. William nodded familiarly to the desk clerk, and the couple turned down the hall to the left. Luckily for me the clerk turned her back to answer the phone as I breezed past her desk and ducked down the hallway. Unluckily, I was just in time to hear the elevator door close and an apartment door slam. I didn't know whether they had gone up, down, or remained on the main floor. There were about twenty doors on the main floor, which meant we had "narrowed" the search to one hundred apartments.

Back outside, Jim and I settled down for what we figured would be a long wait, but in five minutes William came back out alone, slid into his car and drove slowly off to his home.

Was this a sexy boss-secretary affair, or merely a platonic father-daughter relationship? Had we found an example of that rare species, the clean old man?

On Wednesday I went back to visit Dorothy. She ushered me into the library and pressed $300 in crisp bills into my hand.

"Bingo?" I asked.

"Of course," she replied.

She showed me two tickets she had found in William's desk for a play at the Arena Stage the following night.

"He knows I'll be out," she said. "Tuesdays and Thursdays are Bingo nights."

Jim and I enjoyed the play. We had an excellent view both of the stage and of William and his lovely Pakistani import as they held hands during the show. We followed them back to the apartment building, which was kept locked at night. The girl opened the door with a key, they both entered, and the door slammed shut in my face. We hustled around to the left side of the building in time to see a light flick on in a main-floor apartment that jutted out in an alcove facing the street. Once again we settled down for a long wait.

And once again William left after five minutes! I was beginning to trust my early intuition that the man was too decrepit to be anyone's lover. But what was William up to? If they were platonic friends, why was he hiding the relationship from Dorothy? And underlying all the questions about William was one about Dorothy—would her Bingo luck hold out long enough for us to figure out William's game?

He followed the same pattern twice more the next week. The mystery of his relationship with the girl deepened as we watched them together. They seemed more like father and daughter than lovers. Either William was not interested in the girl's sexual potential (which seemed difficult to believe) or he was a cagy adulterer, indeed.

The first real break in the case came on a Thursday afternoon when Dorothy phoned me before she left for the firehouse. She said that William had been called out of town on an important emergency assignment and told her he would return on Monday. Who comes home from a business trip on *Monday?*

I have seen many an adulterer who is super-careful when he is involved in his normal routines. But, when he has convinced the spouse he is out of town, chances are the adulterer will go to town. I felt we had a good chance of catching William in Georgetown over the weekend.

Friday night, all day Saturday and Sunday morning Jim

and I twiddled our thumbs as we watched the apartment from our cars. Nothing happened. The girl went shopping—alone. She returned—alone.

We were about ready to assume that Dorothy had wasted her Bingo money when an airport cab pulled up at the apartment door. William Preston emerged, suitcase in hand, and strolled leisurely into the lobby.

The weekend desk clerk left the lobby door unlocked and he paid no attention as two detectives followed William down the hall. Our subject turned into the front alcove and we stepped out of sight around the corner.

He knocked on the door of the apartment we had spotted, and we heard a female voice coo, "Honey, is that you?"

As the door opened I peeked around the corner and caught a quick glimpse of them kissing. It was no daughterly peck on the cheek. He went inside and I moved down the hall to tape the door.

As I leaned over to insert the matchstick I could hear the girl talking with William. The thin walls gave them little privacy, but they seemed unconcerned.

"Honey," the girl called. "I'm going to hop into the shower. Why don't you pull the bed down?"

At that point in the conversation I decided it was worth the risk of hanging around in the hallway. I heard an old hideaway bed being pulled down from the wall. Then I listened to the sounds of a shower, and what seemed to be a little game of slap and tickle. I heard muffled giggling. Then I listened as the bedsprings began to squeak in earnest.

Meanwhile Jim found a side entrance to the building. He jammed paper into the latch so that it would not lock from the outside. Using that convenient entrance one or the other of us was able to check the tape every fifteen minutes for the entire night. It remained undisturbed. From the outside we could witness that the lights were off. That's proof enough for any judge.

During the night I also sneaked down to the lobby and

checked the bulletin board, where I found a notice which named several tenants. One of them was Diana Norris. The gorgeous girl from Pakistan and William's "nice little secretary" were one and the same.

Dorothy nearly went into shock when we presented our report, but Lou Shaeffer, her attorney, tried to get her to appear calm as he prepared the case for court. He cautioned her not to reveal our investigation to her husband, but some of her agitation must have shown through. William grew nervous and made yet another mistake. He rented an apartment nearby and moved out of the house, taking only a single suitcase.

To prepare for a divorce trial the attorney needed an evaluation of all the jointly owned property, so he hired an art appraiser to visit the Preston home and study the hundreds of pieces of precious art and sculpture. The appraiser's report estimated the total value of the collection at something more than $300,000.

Lou and I visited Dorothy that afternoon and gently reminded her that she had fallen behind in her payments to both of us.

"After Bingo," she said with an air of assurance.

Lou suggested she might sell off one or two art pieces, but she brushed the idea aside, claiming that everything had sentimental value. What was sentimental, we wanted to know, about statues and pottery?

Dorothy, in tears, finally admitted that all the pieces had been brought into the country illegally. With his government connections William had been able to whisk through customs without so much as a hint of inspection. Over the years he had assembled a fortune in smuggled art. Dorothy had known of the scheme and feared prosecution as his accomplice.

Now I could understand why a gorgeous young woman would sleep with William. I had little doubt that the girl's apartment was also adorned with luxurious and illicit art objects.

Now, too, I suspected that Dorothy's "Bingo money" was really the profits from a few back-room art sales.

While Lou discussed details of the divorce proceedings with Dorothy, I snooped around William's files. Behind two cabinets was a heavy brown briefcase. It was locked.

"William never allowed me to see in there," Dorothy explained. "He said it was top secret."

Back in my office I picked the lock and examined the contents. They were top secret, all right, but they were William's secrets, not the government's. True, there was a thick file folder of government travel orders and job descriptions, but none were classified. One of my investigators, who formerly worked for the Central Intelligence Agency, looked at the documents and pointed out such mysterious items as authorization for William, a civilian, to work in an Army uniform; travel orders which showed numerous short trips to Korea, Japan, South Vietnam; unexplained vouchers of payments made and received. My associate said he had no doubt that William was a secret agent, probably for the CIA.

But other materials in the briefcase gave evidence that William liked to pursue more than diplomatic relations. There were photographs of young, beautiful Oriental girls. There were love letters from women thanking William for gifts of cash and jewels. There was a letter from a friend at the United States Aid Mission to Liberia, inviting William to come visit the country because "there are beaucoup girls from Germany, Sweden, the United States, just panting for a man. . . ."

Some spy, this William!

Then I came across a canceled check that William had written on June 27, 1947, payable to cash in the amount of $750. The back of the check had been pasted over with cardboard. My secretary keeps a spray iron at the office to touch up her clothes if she happens to be out all night with her boss—on an investigation. I plugged in the iron, sprayed the back of the check, and heated the ancient glue to loosen bits of the cardboard. Finally I could read the unsigned message scrawled onto the back in a feminine handwriting:

"I want this much a month from now on."

Back in 1947 William supposedly worked for the Civil Service Commission at a modest salary of $5,900 a year, but someone had been squeezing him for nearly twice that amount. The briefcase gave no hint as to how, or if, William paid off the extortionist. But it seemed obvious that he had long been a man of many dark secrets.

We had little faith that such a hustler would continue to allow Dorothy to guard $300,000 worth of smuggled art. As a precaution, Lou obtained a court order restraining William from removing any item from the house.

Nervous days passed before the case was scheduled to go to court. Unable to stand the tension by herself, Dorothy went to visit her sister for a few days. I assigned Jim to keep an eye on the house. Sure enough, the very first morning Dorothy was gone the pink Plymouth crawled up the street, followed by a huge yellow moving van. Jim called me . . . I called Lou . . . Lou called the sheriff . . . and before William even unlocked the house he was slapped with the restraining order. William read it slowly, then turned an even deeper shade of red than normal as Lou told him that we knew about the smuggling scheme. Lou threatened William with exposure if he made another try for the art.

In court both William and Diana admitted the details of our investigation—except for the adultery. They claimed they had spent the night together without engaging in sexual intercourse. The judge listened carefully to our testimony, took a close look at Diana, and granted Dorothy an immediate divorce on grounds of adultery. To everyone's relief, the subject of art appreciation never came up in court.

Within a few days William resigned his job and

disappeared. A month later Dorothy received a card from her ex-husband, saying hello and informing her that he was all right. The card was postmarked Addis Ababa, Ethiopia.

He did not mention Diana, but she undoubtedly was with him. Nor did he mention the $300,000 worth of smuggled art, which, to this day, is guarded by a nervous, aging woman who plays Bingo every Tuesday and Thursday night.

4

STUNG BY A STINGRAY

There is a certain breed of car whose function is not simply to get the driver from one place to another, but to get some attractive young chick to go with him. The make of the automobile is less important than its array of accessories: mag wheels, superwide tires, a raucous muffler, rear-deck spoiler and a tape deck.

Such a car is known as a "pussywagon." It attracts some women, but it also attracts attention. For the adulterer, a dull-looking Ford is a better idea.

If a private detective is on your tail he'll probably be driving a rather ordinary small car. It will have a deceptively high-powered engine hidden under the hood, and may have blinking red lights behind the grille and possibly an emergency siren to blast through traffic like an unmarked police car—but your tail probably won't use them to follow you through a stoplight.

He will go out of his way, in fact, to stay out of your way, because if you suspect you are being followed the detective's investigation is blown. If he runs into trouble he will probably just drive away, let you have your fun, and try to catch you another night.

There was a surgeon from a little Pennsylvania town who knew all the tricks of driving to keep from being followed. He eluded me night after night, but in the end he was trapped by his pussywagon.

There were three loves in Dr. Maury Austin's hectic life. The first was his wife, Audrey, an attractive, soft-spoken woman of forty-three who had worked hard to put Maury through college and medical school, and then helped him set up a small-town practice. After bearing three children she was still slim and petite. But her handsome husband, who was six years younger, apparently lost interest in her once he began earning his own money.

The second love was a well-built brunette nurse we will call Ginny. Ginny assisted Dr. Austin in the operating room at the local hospital. He soon began to operate on her.

Maury's third love was a brand-new Corvette Stingray with chrome-plated tailpipes and a glossy yellow paint job. Maury kept it hidden in the garage except for special occasions. Normally he zoomed back and forth between his office and the hospital in a simple MG roadster.

The Austin marriage was terminally ill, but for months Audrey refused to recognize the symptoms. After one particularly bitter bedroom quarrel Audrey dragged her pillow to the basement couch, which became her bed for the next lonely eight months.

Two events brought about the final crisis of the marriage. One evening Maury received a telephone call at home, told Audrey that he had been summoned to the hospital for emergency surgery, hopped into his MG and drove off. An hour later the hospital called. An astonished Audrey took the message that an emergency case had just come in and Maury was needed at the hospital for surgery. When she later confronted him with his lie, Maury claimed he *was* at the hospital and someone had made a mistake.

Someone had!

Then there was the hospital gossip. One of the nurses walked into a surgical-supply room and discovered a certain doctor and nurse kissing passionately. The juicy story circulated quickly among the hospital staff until it reached the ears of a clerk in the personnel office—who happened to be the doctor's mother-in-law.

Audrey decided to hire a private detective. She was afraid to trust anyone local but she spotted my name in the Washington, D.C., yellow pages. At a lunch she poured out her story and tearfully asked me to investigate. Though the Austins were quite well off financially, Maury kept a tight hold on the cash. Audrey had managed to borrow a few hundred dollars from her mother, and she asked if I could keep my fee to a minimum.

Most detectives don't like to take on a case for a small retainer. Like anything else in life, you get what you pay for, and a thorough investigation is an expensive investigation. But I'm a sucker for a woman's tears, and with some disbelief I heard myself suggesting that I could do some preliminary work alone. Only when I was sure we could prove adultery would I bring in an assistant.

That evening I was parked down the block from Dr. Austin's house when he ran out, jumped into his MG and drove off. I followed him to the hospital and waited outside for a couple of hours. When he left the hospital shortly after ten he headed in the direction of the Maryland border—directly away from his home. There were few cars on the road this late at night, so I had to follow at a discreet distance to avoid alarming him.

The MG disappeared for a moment as my car nosed upward to cross a railroad bridge, and as I drove back down the other side I saw it parked off the road. The doctor was being very cautious. I had no choice but to drive past him. About a half mile up the road I found a darkened gas station, where I parked, turned off my lights and waited. A few minutes later Maury sped by. Again I eased behind him at a safe distance and followed for about fifteen miles as he began to wind up into the mountain country.

At a dark crossroads he pulled into the parking lot of an abandoned diner, and once again I was forced to drive casually on by. Up the road I waited for ten minutes before returning to the intersection. The MG had disappeared.

Muttering to myself, I began to drive the back roads that forked off at the intersection. Dirt pathways with deep ruts and sticky mud puddles wound up and down the mountains. Barking dogs greeted me at isolated farmhouses. Dilapidated tarpaper shacks and a few new brick homes were tucked nearly out of sight. Nowhere could I spot a trace of Maury's MG. After two frustrating hours I gave up for the night.

Two nights later—a Wednesday—I tried again. This time I felt ready to outsmart the careful surgeon. When he left the hospital parking lot I zoomed ahead of him and sped to the country intersection where I had lost him previously. I found a spot where I could back my car off the road and still have a good view of the crossroad. Soon the MG appeared and the cautious driver once again waited at the intersection for about five minutes. Then he gunned his MG into life and turned down the road to the right.

As soon as he was out of sight I started down the road after him. From my search two nights earlier I knew the road reached a three-way fork about a half mile from the highway. I was afraid I might lose him again so I put my poor Ford through torture. Bouncing crazily along the path, bumping my head on the roof of the car, banging my knees against the steering column, I raced toward the fork. As I careened around a bend I almost hit the MG, parked at the fork with Maury in it, patiently waiting to see if anyone was following!

What could I do? I chose one of the three roads and bounced my way past him without hesitation, hoping that he would believe I was merely a neighbor on my way home.

It was a mile or so before I could find a spot to turn around. Creeping back to the fork, I wasn't surprised to discover that Maury had disappeared once again. For two more hours I searched and searched. My car found a lot of mudholes, but I couldn't find any dirt on Maury.

As I took my Ford through the car wash the next day I began to get really mad. I had just phoned Audrey, and she almost called me a liar. She just couldn't believe that Maury had got away from me twice. She was so upset that she accused me of pocketing her money and not doing my job. I cursed her tears that had persuaded me to take the case, and I promised Audrey that Maury would not get away the third time.

Why do I say things like that?

On Friday night I was parked at my hiding place near the same intersection when Maury played his little waiting game with the MG. Once again he sped off down the right-hand road. It was difficult to hold back, but I had to give Maury five minutes or so to park at the fork. Finally my impatience got the better of me and I eased down the bumpy road.

As I rounded a curve two headlights blasted my eyes, and I had to throw my car into a ditch to avoid being hit by Maury's onrushing MG. He was heading back to the main road!

Employing every curse I had ever heard, and inventing some new ones, I raced around the curve on foot, hoping to catch a glimpse of Maury's path. I spotted the MG as it paused for a moment and then hopped *across* the highway to the *other side* of the intersection! It sped off out of sight down a country lane.

It took me twenty minutes to escape from the muddy ditch. In vain I inspected the houses on the other side of the highway for the MG. Disgusted with myself, I drove the long way home.

What was I going to tell my client?

As I neared home, exhausted, I hit upon a plan of action.

The next day I called Audrey. "Listen, I have some bad news for you," I said.

"What?"

"I couldn't go out on your case last night," I lied. "I got

called out on a big investigation we've been working on for months. Sorry. When do you think he might go off again?"

"Well . . . he usually spends the weekend with the kids. Probably Monday."

"Okay. I'll try Monday."

By this time I had lost all objectivity about the case. Dr. Maury Austin was no longer the mere subject of an adultery investigation. He was the prey and I was the hunter. I was determined to pin an adultery rap on him.

I had two choices of action. I could try to bug his car with a beeper that would signal his location to me. That would be risky. The little black boxes cost nearly $500 apiece and there was no guarantee that the magnetic attachments would hold up against the punishment of the back-country roads. And neither of Maury's cars was designed to accommodate the beeper. It would have been visible from the rear of the MG, and as for the Stingray, how do you get a magnet to stick to the car's fiberglass body?

The other alternative was to bring in additional manpower, and I chose this course. Without telling Audrey (and without charging her) I would bring a second investigator and a second car onto the job. I was convinced that, working together and communicating via our two-way radios, we could catch Maury this time.

Audrey told me Maury had to make hospital rounds about 5 P.M., and said he would be home late. So we staked out the hospital parking lot in the afternoon, and when Maury arrived I felt sure we were going to catch him that night.

He had driven the Stingray! Some wild impulse had given him the notion to risk his beautiful toy on the back-country lanes. He didn't know it, but he was risking his marriage, his home and his considerable personal fortune at the same time.

As soon as Maury left the hospital and drove off in the same familiar direction, we raced on ahead. Jack Fogerty and I, in separate cars, were waiting for him—hidden on both sides of the intersection.

Passion, apparently, got the better of Maury that night. The same impulse that caused him to drive the Stingray instead of the MG also caused him to forget about waiting at the side of the road. When he reached the intersection he immediately sped off to the left, past my hiding place and down a country lane.

Ten minutes later Jack joined me and I pointed to the lane. "He's down there. Let's go find the son of a bitch."

The lane rambled along and forked off in two different directions. Jack went to the right and I went to the left. Slowly, with our headlights off, we cruised along looking for the Stingray.

Like a yellow submarine shining in the moonlight, the Stingray protruded from the rear of a new brick house. I had passed the house many times before, but Maury had been able to do a better job of hiding the MG. I called Jack on my radio, and he came to join me.

The house was in a cluster of three, but it was the only one occupied. The name on the mailbox was Virginia Baker—we knew her as Ginny. I wrote down the name and number of the realtor listed on the "For Sale" signs in front of the other two homes.

Because the area was so isolated, and perhaps because Maury's sudden carelessness had rubbed off on his lover, only a thin set of sheer curtains covered the window. Jack and I sneaked up behind some bushes and watched the doctor examine his patient. We took careful notes.

Now the case was set, and we only had a few details to clean up. I was curious as to whether the girl was renting her new home or whether someone else had paid for it. So the next day I called the realtor and told him I had seen three homes back in the country. I asked if all three were for sale. He told me that two were for sale, but that one was already sold. I thanked him, hung up, and headed for the courthouse to check the land deeds. The owner of record was a certain Dr. Maury Austin.

As it turned out, Maury was fortunate he had bought the modest little home in the backwoods. Audrey demanded and won a huge settlement to keep the scandal out of the local courts. She got their home and hefty alimony and child-support payments too.

Today Maury lives in the little house with his new bride. They drive to the hospital together each morning in a dark blue Volkswagen.

5

PARTY IN
PRINCE WILLIAM PARK

Ralph Armstrong watched his wife dress for work. As she pulled a stocking over her shapely right leg, she did not seem to notice the streak of clear nail polish he had painted on the nylon.

When she returned home at 3 A.M. that November morning, Ralph pretended to be asleep. Through barely open eyelids he watched Betty undress and peel the marked stocking from her *left* leg!

Ralph sat up in bed and called her a bitch. Once more the couple leaped into one of their loud, vicious fights. Once more their neighbors in the enlisted men's apartments called the Military Police. And once more the troops had to separate the pair and restore quiet to the residential neighborhood on the Quantico, Virginia, Marine Corps base.

By the time the fight ended Ralph was already late for his duty. With quivering hands he pulled on his green fatigues and drove to his assigned barracks to wake up his troops.

The tension of the past few months was taking a severe toll of the Marine drill instructor. His spit and polish was dull and dirty. His self-discipline had given way to self-pity. His comfortable, regimented life was splitting open.

I have seen hundreds of men and women try to contend

with an adulterous spouse. Owing, I believe, to the enormous importance that our society attaches to sexual faithfulness, the innocent party in a marriage often suffers unimaginable tortures. I have observed countless clients sink into deep depression. They cannot sleep, they consume huge quantities of cigarettes, liquor and tranquilizers, they can't do their work and are often fired as a result.

Sometimes they even go crazy.

Ralph was one of the worst emotional wrecks ever to walk into my office. He came one afternoon after stopping at the credit union to withdraw his life's savings. Despite the fact that he was still in love with Betty the incident with the marked stocking had convinced him that, for the sake of his sanity, he must give his wife a divorce for Christmas.

A tall, solidly-built man of thirty-four, Ralph would have been handsome if his hair had not been shaved in the skinhead style of the Marines. He told me his story in a nervous, high-pitched voice.

His wife Betty was tall and reasonably attractive—perhaps more sexy than beautiful. She worked nights as a cocktail waitress at one of the clubs on the Marine base. Though the club closed at 1 A.M., Betty often did not arrive home until hours later. Sometimes she came back to the apartment with torn clothes or with a dishonorable discharge on her panties. Each time she appeared in such a state Ralph began one of the violent arguments that would bring the MPs running.

Literally dripping with the evidence, Betty readily admitted that she had a lover, but she would not tell Ralph his identity, and that seemed to enrage him more than her unfaithfulness.

Chain-smoking throughout our interview, Ralph ordered me to find the man. He handed me all his money and said he could get more from his parents.

I warned him that the investigation would be both difficult and risky. It is illegal to conduct surveillance upon a military base without first getting the permission of the Criminal Investigation Division (CID). But how could I confide in the MPs when one of their men might be Betty's lover?

It is also *extremely* illegal to carry a firearm onto a military base without permission, but I had little desire to find myself cornered by a huge jungle fighter without the protection of my gun. We decided to risk the wrath of the MPs and proceed secretly to find Betty's lover. At the slightest suspicion that anyone was aware of our presence we would call off the surveillance and resume it another night.

Quantico is a huge military base located off U.S. Route 1 between Washington and Richmond. Hundreds of miles of isolated roadways wind across the base, leading to scores of possible hideaways, and it was going to be difficult to follow Betty unnoticed. Luckily one of the cars in our office fleet happened to be a green Rambler, and all the plainclothes CID investigators at Quantico drove green Ramblers. We decided to use that as our main surveillance vehicle.

Communications between the Rambler and a second car presented another problem. We suspected that the CID regularly monitored short-wave radio frequencies near the base, and we were afraid to give away our presence by talking on the car radios. We were forced to use limited-range walkie-talkies. For the same reason we dared not place an electronic beeper on Betty's black Pontiac lest the MPs pick up the signal.

There was, however, one visual signal we could use. As we staked out the club on the first night of our surveillance, I grabbed a screwdriver, casually walked over to Betty's car in the parking lot, and jammed it through the red plastic cover of her left taillight. This produced a pinhole through which white light would shine like a star. Betty would now be easier to follow from a distance.

Cautiously we tracked her from the club at 1 A.M. We could follow only for short distances on the winding roads without appearing obvious. After several nights we became familiar with the pattern of her driving, and we stationed ourselves further along the route. Finally, we tracked her to an enlisted men's barracks only a few blocks from the FBI training academy. A dark shadow ran from the barracks and climbed into her car. Carefully we followed them out the main gate and north on U.S. Route 1.

They pulled into a gas station, and as I drove past I saw a Marine climb out and walk toward the restroom. I slowed down to look. He was only about five feet eight, but he was built like a grizzly bear.

I waited along the side of the road while Jack Fogerty took over and tracked the white pinpoint of light down the straight highway to the entrance of Prince William Forest Park. Supposedly the park was closed at night, and Jack did not want to arouse suspicion by roaring in after the couple, so he radioed his position to me and waited.

I picked Jack up in my car and made the Rambler invisible by turning off the headlights and flicking the special switch on the dashboard that keeps the stoplights from flashing when the brakes are applied. We drove into the park. Silent and unseen, the car eased along the hilly roads in search of our subjects.

Down a pathway to the left we spotted a match flickering in the darkness, followed by the soft orange glow of two smokers as they sat in their car. We dared not approach too closely, but sat for more than an hour watching the darkened car. As 3 A.M. neared, the car started up and left. We let them go and went over to examine the parking spot. We collected cigarette butts, an empty Marlboro pack, coffee cups and Twinkie wrappers.

By itself this trash would hardly be conclusive evidence, but we always gather every available scrap that can help substantiate our testimony. This is one of the details that most detectives ignored, as I observed them for five years from my bailiff's bench.

The next afternoon Jack and I were back in the park,

blazing a trail from U.S. 1 through the woods to the lovers' parking space. Cold, gusty winds made the job downright unpleasant. The weather was even worse later that night as I huddled behind a tree with my walkie-talkie and binoculars.

Betty and her beau arrived about 1:30 in the morning, just as I was seriously beginning to worry about frostbite. Jack followed them to the park, left his car up on the highway and hiked through the deepening snow to join me.

By the time Jack arrived I was glued to the binoculars. Betty was crawling all over the big Marine, kissing and caressing him with abandon. Their hot breath fogged the car windows but the infrared lenses of the binoculars cut through the haze.

Betty disappeared from view for about ten minutes. Her lover began writhing in ecstasy, and then he disappeared, too. Slowly at first, then wildly, the parked car began to rock back and forth. A squeaking spring broke the stillness of the snowy night.

Afterward the lovers smoked, drank coffee and ate a snack. Once again they heaved the trash out the window, blissfully unaware that it might be thrown into their faces in court.

Ralph met me in my office the next day and put his fist through a window pane when I told him the story. He lapsed into sobs as my secretary bandaged his hand.

"I can't believe it," he moaned. "I just can't believe it."

I showed him the trash. He had not told me what brand of cigarette Betty smoked, but he stared solemnly at the empty pack of Marlboros.

I had checked the names of the men who lived in the barracks, and there were only three who would use the particular door we had been watching. I reviewed the names with Ralph to see if we could single out one man. When I mentioned Richard O'Neil, Ralph started.

"Betty has talked about him," he said. "He's a big hero on the football team."

(Later I picked up a copy of the Quantico newspaper. In the sports section was a photograph of Richard O'Neil, who had scored the winning touchdown in a game with Fort Meade, Maryland. It was not his only score, for he was the man we had spotted as Betty's lover.)

Adultery in a car is difficult to prove. Since space is limited, especially for a burly football player, a judge is reluctant to believe that sexual intercourse actually occurred. My tactic, as usual, is to build up a mountain of evidence so enormous that it cannot be ignored in court. My best cases, in fact, usually never make it that far. The majority of subjects that I have caught in the act choose to settle their divorces out of court, making generous concessions rather than see the details of their escapades bared in public.

When Ralph muttered threats against Betty and her boyfriend, I explained that we needed more evidence and that any temperamental action on his part now would hurt the case.

He eyed me suspiciously and said, "Are you sure you're telling me the truth about this? I just can't believe it!"

I made allowances for the fact that Ralph was under stress. If he did not believe me, there was one sure way to convince him.

"Get yourself a babysitter for tomorrow night," I said. "You're going on an investigation with me."

When Betty left work we followed carefully. I showed Ralph the white pinpoint of light on the back of her car. We eased along a parallel road as Betty drove away with her lover, but suddenly she gunned the car down a side road and disappeared.

I was stunned. How could I lose her on this night—when I was out to prove myself to her husband? Betty had never used that road before. We could find no trace of her.

"Well, I think I know where they are," I said and drove to Prince William Park. We left the car on the highway and tramped through the woods to the love nest. It was empty. We waited in vain for half an hour.

"I know where they might be," Ralph volunteered. "There's a parking area on the base where couples can go. The MPs don't bother them."

"Let's try it."

Ralph directed me back to the base, to a secluded spot up a long, hilly dead-end drive. We sat at the deserted lovers' lane, trying to figure out our next move. While we were up there I radioed to Jim Metz to ask about another investigation.

As I turned the green Rambler around to head back down the hill, suddenly, out of nowhere, the road was blocked by *another* green Rambler with flashing red lights. A jeep pulled up to join it. Then another. And another. A second green Rambler joined the group. All were flashing their harsh beacons in our faces.

"What are we going to do?" Ralph moaned in his high-pitched voice. "My God, what are we going to do?"

We couldn't run; we could only bluff. I unbuckled my gun holster and threw it under the seat. "Let me do the talking," I said, and I eased the car down the hill.

"Halt!" boomed a voice from the darkness.

The five vehicles drew around the car like Indians encircling a wagon train. A skinhead in a business suit walked up to the window.

"What are you doing?" he demanded to know.

"Jeeeeesus Christ, mister!" I drawled. "I'm trying to find my way off this base. How the hell do I get to the road to Fredericksburg?"

I had no chance to see if my ploy would work, for Ralph opened his mouth. "We're lost, *sir,*" he squeaked. "We just can't find our way out of here, *sir!*"

The CID man looked over at my passenger. Ralph's haircut left little doubt as to his military status, and his girlish voice seemed to answer the question as to what two men were doing up on a lovers' lane at 2 A.M. With a disgusted look the CID man commanded, "Follow us."

They drove us in convoy fashion to the MP headquarters, where I asked to see the chief in private. In his office I flashed my identification.

"Look, I'm a private detective," I explained. "You can call the state police to verify it. This guy—I guess you know him—has a problem with his wife—and I guess you know that, too. I'm doing an investigation for him and his attorney. His wife's been running around, and we know who the man is."

"Yea," the chief replied. "I think I know, too."

"We've already got a lot of evidence on her and I think we can wrap up the case tonight."

The chief thought for a moment. "Okay," he said. "It looks all right. One thing, though . . . do you have a gun with you?"

"No, sir," I lied. "I know I can't carry a gun onto a military base. You can search my car if you want to."

"No, that won't be necessary."

He let us go, but by the time I drove Ralph home he was shaking uncontrollably. Tears streamed down the face of the tough Marine drill instructor.

The next day, babbling incoherently, Ralph was sent to Bethesda Navy Medical Center and placed on the psychiatric ward. He called me a couple of days later, calmed down a bit by tranquilizers, and told me he still wanted me to continue the surveillance. He had decided to carry the case to the bitter end and was even thinking of fighting for custody of the two children.

It was a Monday. Betty was off work that night, and with Ralph in the hospital we suspected she would take advantage of her freedom, so we staked out the apartment house in the afternoon. Snow was falling, and the roads were beginning to freeze.

She left the house, and I followed in my car with a new assistant I'll call Judy Mallory. Betty headed for Bethesda Navy Medical Center, and we waited in the parking lot while she visited with Ralph. Darkness was falling when she emerged from the hospital entrance accompanied by a man in a bathrobe. Peering through the infrared binoculars I could see that Ralph was walking her to her car. Heads bobbed vigorously as though in argument. Suddenly Ralph grabbed his wife and with a vicious backhanded slap knocked her against a tree. She pulled herself to her feet and ran for her car while Ralph watched her go.

Betty drove quickly up Wisconsin Avenue and turned onto the Capitol Beltway. By now the roads were treacherous. Through a blinding snowstorm Betty kept her foot planted on the gas pedal. My speedometer registered eighty-five miles an hour as I tried to keep up. Suddenly my Rambler fishtailed, spun around and slid toward the side of the road. Judy screamed. We glided to a stop half off the road, our car turned backward to face the oncoming traffic.

Carefully I turned around and drove back toward Quantico at a sane forty miles an hour. Even at that speed I had trouble maintaining control, and we both kept a careful watch, fully expecting to find a black Pontiac wrapped around a tree.

Betty's car was not at the apartment, nor at the officers' Club, nor at the enlisted men's barracks. I wondered if she was going to report Ralph's attack, so I checked the MP station, but the car was not there either.

Could she have been crazy enough to go to the park in this weather?

We drove to the park entrance. There, covered lightly by the falling snow, a fresh set of tire tracks pointed the way inside. Turning off my lights, I drove along the now-familiar park roads and managed to sneak up on their retreat, stopping the car at a safe distance. Our footsteps muffled by the snow, Judy and I crept toward the black Pontiac. As we approached, the car once again began to rock back and forth. Boldly (my gun was strapped onto my belt) we ventured close and peeked inside.

For twenty minutes Judy and I witnessed the act of adultery as the car continued to sway. Finally it quieted down and we moved back behind a tree.

The lovers took a pizza box from the back seat and munched away, washing the cold food down with coffee. Then they heaved the trash out the car window and drove off, leaving two detectives to clean up after them. A few minutes later we put the evidence into our car, started the engine—and spun our wheels.

All night long we slipped and slid. We gathered branches and twigs for traction. We pushed. We pulled. We gunned the engine forward. We jammed it into reverse. If Judy had not begun to cry hysterically, we might have found a good way to keep warm for the night, but I find it difficult to make a pass at a sobbing woman. Finally, as the sun was rising over the forest trees, I got smart, let half the air out of the tires and managed to crawl up to the main highway and head for home.

Only to find that all our work was in vain.

Poor Ralph continued to deteriorate, and doctors committed him to a psychiatric hospital with a poor prognosis for a cure. Betty moved out of town shortly afterward, with the two children.

Bags of trash from the parties in Prince William Park remain carefully preserved in my files.

6

FAST COMPANY

She took my change and walked over to the jukebox. The money clanked into the slot and she pressed several buttons. She walked drunkenly back toward me, took my right hand and pulled it around her waist.

"I picked slow numbers," she said teasingly.

We danced, and she pressed her whole body tightly up against mine. I lifted her face up toward mine and kissed her. I wanted her to remember me when we met again in court.

It all began when an attorney called me to handle the case of Bernie Emmons, who had moved out of his home in Charles Town, West Virginia, a few months earlier. Bernie, a quiet, hard-working government employee, had watched a sudden, drastic change come over his wife, Margie, after ten years of marriage. She lost interest in the two children and in him. She went out with her girlfriends and dragged back home at two or three in the morning, drunk and disheveled. While she lied to Bernie at first, she soon grew bold enough to flaunt her sexual affairs at him.

Margie Emmons is not a pretty woman. Her body is well proportioned, but her face is rather ordinary and she wears severe dark-rimmed glasses. Nevertheless, she became quite a hit with the menfolk who frequented the country bars in the area.

Eventually Bernie filed for a formal separation. Under the terms of the agreement Margie was to have custody of the children, allowing her husband reasonable visitation rights. Bernie was to pay Margie $200 a month in child support. He soon realized, however, that Margie would not settle for that sum. She called him nearly every day to demand that he pay for car repairs, items for the home, clothes for the boys.

Bernie missed his sons badly. Weekend visits were a poor substitute for the close relationship he had once enjoyed with them. He longed to have them back, and decided to fight for them.

His attorney warned him that child-custody battles are difficult for a father to win. They generally require a double-barreled approach. First, the husband must prove a flagrant—perhaps promiscuous—case of adultery against his wife. But even that may not be sufficient, for he must also convince the court that he can offer the children a good home with responsible day care.

Bernie's case looked good on both counts. First, because Margie flaunted her sexual behavior so openly; and second, because Bernie's mother agreed to testify that she would live with Bernie and care for the children.

By the time I entered the case it sounded simple. If Margie was running around as much as Bernie claimed, she would be easy to catch. What I didn't realize was that Margie ran with some very fast company. She had fallen in with a stock-car-racing crowd, and no one in the group confined his racing to the track.

Bernie gave us the names of several men that Margie had bragged about. Armed with this information we staked out the subject's home that same evening. She left the house about 7:30 and took the two children to a babysitter. Then she turned her car onto the main highway and accelerated like a jet leaving the runway. She drove between eighty and ninety miles an hour on a two-lane country highway that wound up and down the mountains. She careened around curves, often straying dangerously across the yellow line. In only a few moments we lost her, for it would have been impossible to follow her without arousing suspicion.

We had to reconsider our plans. We could not install a beeper for it would never remain in place when Margie took the highway bumps at ninety miles an hour. But while she was at work the next day we did employ our technique of puncturing her left taillight.

It didn't help. The next couple of weeks became a nightmare for us as we tried to chase Margie without blowing our cover. To this day I don't understand how she managed to control her car. There seemed to be a good chance Bernie would gain custody of the children by default if he could only wait until Margie plunged her car off a bridge or wrapped it around a tree.

My assistant, Guy Morgan, and I followed her every Friday, Saturday and Sunday night for weeks. Gradually we were able to develop a pattern of her route. One of us would station himself further along the route each night in an attempt to learn her destination, but her maniac-style driving allowed us to follow for only brief distances each time. Progress was slow.

Every time we lost her we would cruise around to the country bars looking in vain for her car. We checked the local stock-car race track, but could not find her. It was a dull, frustrating case.

Finally, on a Saturday night after we had once again lost her, we returned to Margie's home to await her arrival. At 12:45 A.M. a black Mercury pulled up at the house. We had never seen it before, nor had we seen the driver, who waited somewhat impatiently in front of the house. After fifteen minutes he drove off, tires squealing.

Forty minutes later he returned, but this time the car was followed by Margie's. She parked her car and hopped into the black Mercury. Once again it sped off, and Guy and I followed as best we could. The Mercury flew around a corner and ran a red light at the main highway. We could not follow, for if we too ran the light it would be a dead giveaway of our presence. Reluctantly, we returned to Margie's home.

About an hour later the black Mercury came back, dropped Margie off, and left. It wasn't much, but it was the first bit of evidence that Margie was indeed meeting a man. And on Monday, when we checked the license-plate number of the black Mercury, we learned that the driver was married.

That remained the only bit of evidence we could gather for weeks.

Guy and I grew weary of the chase. It seemed as if we would never catch the elusive Margie in an incriminating situation. Bernie's money was running low.

Finally Margie herself provided the information we needed. Her passion for torturing Bernie with stories of her sexual adventures was Margie's big mistake. She called him one Thursday to ask if he would watch the children for the weekend. She said she was going to visit some old friends in Pennsylvania, and she made it very plain that she was not going by herself.

When she hung up the phone Bernie removed a cassette from the tape recorder he had attached to the receiver. He brought the tape to my office, and Guy and I made plans for the weekend.

At six Friday evening we arrived at the address supplied to us by Bernie. A dark blue 1970 Corvette Stingray was parked in front of the house.

We waited for hours and observed nothing. Finally about 9 P.M. Margie walked from the house and took a small bag out of the Stingray. She went back inside. Twenty minutes later Margie emerged hand in hand with a man. We assumed he was John Crawford, one of several men Margie liked to brag about, who owned a blue Stingray. Another couple was with them, and they drove off in another car, obviously going out together for Saturday night on the town. We knew we would not catch Margie and John alone, so we waited at the house, guarding the Stingray.

Sitting together for four hours, Guy and I had little to do but share our depression, for it seemed doubtful that the case would break that night. It appeared that Margie and John would simply sleep over at the home of their friends, and with four people in the house we could not prove adultery.

Gloomily we watched the foursome arrive back home about 1 A.M. and enter the house together.

Then, to our delight, Margie and John came back out and hopped into the Stingray. They were drunk. John's car weaved back and forth along the road. Now it didn't matter how fast he might drive, for in their condition they would not spot us. We hung closely onto the tail of the Corvette.

Instead of driving to the interstate that would take them back to Charles Town, John pulled into the parking lot of a local motel. Guy shouted, "Hooo-raay!" into the car radio. I was afraid the light of my smile might give away our presence.

They had apparently already registered, for they simply got out of the car and headed for room 226. Grinning from ear to ear, I sneaked over and taped the door. Guy kept the door under observation while I went to the motel office.

The night clerk was dozing, but he woke up when I entered. I flashed my identification.

"I'm a detective," I informed him.

He glanced briefly at my identification. Most people assume that a detective is with the police, and I never bother to make the distinction unless questioned. The clerk was most helpful. The registration card for room 226 was in the name of Mr. and Mrs. John Crawford (John was not married). The room had been rented for $16 for one night. I thanked the clerk.

"It is very important that you tell no one about our presence," I said. "We are following a certain party, and there will be no trouble here. But you must forget about us."

"Yes sir, yes sir," the room clerk whispered.

Unfortunately the motel offered no room with a good view of room 226, so Guy and I faced a long night of watching from our cars in the parking lot. Periodically we checked the tape on room 226 to establish our evidence of adultery.

In the morning the couple left the motel hand in hand. We took photos to prove it. They drove home about 10 A.M. and we let them go, knowing that we could never follow them on the long drive.

Eagerly I rushed over to the telephone to call the attorney. He was pleased. Bernie was hurt and happy at the same time.

Guy and I drove home for some much-needed sleep, and on Monday we began work on several other cases that had piled up while we were chasing Margie. Our records went into the files awaiting a court date.

But two months later the attorney called me again. He was getting ready to file the case. If this were simply a divorce hearing, we would have ample evidence to win the case. But Bernie was firm in his resolve to fight for custody of the children. If possible, the attorney wanted to document the adultery even further. It would be devastating in court if we could show that Margie was not only an adulteress but a promiscuous one, lavishing her favors on a variety of lovers.

So Guy and I arrived at Margie's home at 8:30 the following Friday evening. Now that we had placed Margie in a motel room with a lover, we could be more bold in gathering evidence, for it was no longer possible to blow the case. Margie's car was gone when we arrived, but we could see movement inside the house.

I called from a nearby phone booth, and a young girl answered.

"Is Margie there?" I asked.

"No, she's not."

"Oh, gee. This is a friend of hers. Do you know where I can find her?"

"Yes," the babysitter replied. "She said she'd be at Harry's Place."

I knew it well from other investigations. Harry's Place is no family restaurant. A country shack that sits back off the road, it had been converted into an intimate bar. A dance floor is jammed in between the bar and a handful of booths, and the jukebox blasts out the latest country and western hits. Inside, the beer flows. Outside, two or three times a night, private arguments are settled with bare knuckles.

The few women who frequent Harry's place are there for one of two purposes—either to sell it or give it away.

Only a half dozen cars were in the lot when Guy and I arrived, but Margie's was one of them. She was sitting in a booth next to a blonde girl who was much better looking. We sat down in the adjoining booth.

Margie was the loudest person in the entire bar. Her comments, mixed with choice profanity, rose above the blare of the jukebox.

Guy and I watched the scene, sipping on our beers. When the music stopped Margie could not bear the silence.

"Hell!" she said. "I'm gonna play some music."

"Here," I said on an impulse. I handed her a quarter.

She looked at me and smiled. "Thanks."

In the course of an hour Margie and her girlfriend danced with four different men. One of them, whom they called Tommy, came over and sat between them in the booth.

Our good mood augmented by the beer we were drinking, Guy and I began to trade dirty jokes with the two women. Tommy didn't like it much, but he was outnumbered.

I gave Margie some quarters and said, "Let's dance." Guy grabbed the other girl and the four of us captured the dance floor. That's when Margie pressed herself against me with abandon. As the dance ended she winked at me.

"Thanks," she said.

But the good-time girl then turned her attentions to Tommy, who was so mad he seemed almost ready to invite us both to the parking lot. Margie eased his anger with a juicy kiss, and the two caressed each other while the blonde girlfriend went off with another fellow.

"See you boys again sometime," Margie called cheerfully as she left the bar with Tommy.

"Sure," we replied.

They left in two cars, and once again it proved impossible to follow them. We went back to Margie's home and waited. Shortly after 1 A.M. the two cars arrived in front of the house. Margie got out of her car and went into Tommy's.

For one hour and ten minutes we watched them kiss and hug passionately. Margie disappeared from view while Tommy sat rigidly behind the wheel. Slowly he began to relax, sliding further down into the seat, his face reflecting the ecstasy of what we could only guess to be oral sex.

The area offered no cover for us to move up closely. We documented the passion as best we could through the binoculars.

We next saw Margie at a commissioner's hearing. Guy and I arrived together with Bernie and his lawyer. Margie was already there, and she naturally turned to see who was arriving. At first she looked at me curiously, then as she remembered me her face screwed up in anger. I took a quarter from my pocket and offered it to her from across the room. She cupped one hand to hide the finger that she flashed at me.

She had put on a bit of weight since the investigation, but both Guy and I were able to identify her with little difficulty. The evidence from our motel surveillance was damaging. Margie blushed as we reported on her passionate scene in the car with Tommy.

Finally Margie took the witness stand in her own defense.

She called us liars, but her testimony could not refute the details of our reports.

Before Bernie's lawyer rose to cross-examine her, Bernie held a whispered conference with him. The attorney then informed the commissioner that his client had noticed that his wife had gained weight—particularly in the stomach. He wanted an explanation.

Margie said that the doctor had diagnosed a tumor. Bernie's attorney asked for a continuance, pending a pregnancy test.

When the court physician certified that Margie was three months pregnant, the commissioner awarded custody of the two boys to their father. Margie gave Bernie an angry look as she marched from the room, but she reserved an even more bitter expression for me.

7

WHAT'S THE BUZZ?

Wiretapping! Bugging! Electronic surveillance! Whatever you call it, listening in on the private conversations of lovers is illegal, immoral—and very lucrative. It is one of the most effective tricks in the private detective's bag.

The Safe Streets Act, which became effective in 1968 (18 U.S.C. S 2512), banned the private detective from tapping certain telephone lines and from bugging most private conversations. Ironically, the law probably has helped the private detective more than it has hurt him, because it caused many adulterers to relax their guard. If a private detective is attempting to prove a case of adultery on you, chances are—despite the law—you will be subjected to some form of electronic eavesdropping.

If possible the surveillance will be within the law. This could include the use of an automobile bumper beeper to aid in tracking your car, or, if the detective can get close enough to you, a pocket tape recorder to document your conversation.

But your telephone messages are the most useful conversations to monitor. That can be done legally only if you or the other party has authorized the tap—and we can't exactly ask you to sign a consent form! It is specifically illegal to snoop on a conversation when no party to the discussion is aware of the tap or bug. The private detective has found a simple way around that prohibition: he ignores it and takes his chances. Lulled into a false sense of security, many adulterers now use their home and office telephones, blissfully unaware of the illegal electronic surveillance that is gathering evidence against them.

The evidence cannot be used in court. But if a detective listens in on the private conversation of two lovers, he can often manage to be in the right location at the right time to catch them at the wrong moment.

Even before the Safe Streets Act, wiretapping was a touchy job. It was legal at that time for anyone to tap a telephone line that was registered in his name. Thus a husband could tap his home phone and listen in on the conversation of his wife, and vice versa. But legal or not, electronic surveillance has always seemed to be disreputable, and some clients absolutely refuse to allow it.

The activity of my ulcer is in direct proportion to the number of wiretap cases I have under way at any given moment. Nevertheless, a wiretap often appears to be the only effective way to break a case.

Josephine Weller came to my office in May of 1971 and asked me to tap her home phone in an attempt to prove adultery against her husband. As she described her domestic situation, it seemed obvious that a wiretap was the best course of action.

Josephine worked at night, assembling electronic circuits for a manufacturing firm near Washington. Her twenty-two-year marriage to Terry Weller was breaking up. A few weeks before she came to see me Josephine had bitched once too often about her husband's loud snoring. Enraged, he grabbed some blankets and moved out of their bedroom to a room in the basement. A few days later he had his own phone installed there, but made the mistake of getting only an extension rather than a separate number. Thus the phone in his room was legally registered to his wife.

One evening the couple had a severe fight just before

Josephine left for work. By the time she arrived at her job at 11 P.M. she wanted to apologize. Before beginning work she called Terry, but the phone was busy. So a half hour later she sneaked away from the assembly line to call again. The phone was still busy.

All night Josephine fed the same dime into a pay phone in a futile attempt to call Terry. Incredibly, the line remained busy all night long. Once Josephine even called the operator to see if the phone was out of order. The operator reported that the line was open in a connection to another number.

Night after night after night the phone was busy. Josephine grew to hate the rhythmic busy signal that blocked her from reaching home. She asked her two teenage sons if they had been using the phone. No, their father had said he would be using it, and they were instructed not to touch it.

Thoughts of divorce had been in Josephine's head for some time, and she finally came to me with a plea to find out who her husband was talking to all night long.

There was, of course, only one way to accomplish that.

I met her at her home during the day while Terry was at his job and the kids were in school. Beginning at the phone in Terry's basement bedroom, I traced the telephone wire up into the ceiling of the room and from there to a wall on the main floor where the wire ran next to a ventilating grate. Splicing into the line, I attached the green and yellow "voice" wire to a small black box, only a couple of inches square. The red "hot" wire from the telephone was also attached to another connection in the black box.

The box, plugged to a cassette tape recorder, was hidden inside the ventilator grate and armed with a thirty-minute tape. When a phone receiver was lifted anywhere in the house it would activate the tape and record any conversation. While the message couldn't be used in court, I hoped to find out who, if anyone, was Terry's lover, and when and where I could catch them together.

The little black boxes are easy to get. Once a private detective is listed in the yellow pages he finds himself swamped with mail-order advertisements for a variety of legal and illegal materials. The black box that I installed in Josephine's phone is easy to use because it hooks up to a recorder and does not require constant monitoring.

I carefully taught Josephine how to remove and replace the tape cassettes without disturbing the equipment. We set up a rendezvous in the parking lot of a local motel where we could listen together to any taped messages.

The following afternoon Josephine arrived at the motel and climbed nervously into my car with a tape cassette in her hand. She clenched her fists as I placed the message in my recorder. We heard the receiver lift, and then a number was dialed. When a woman's voice answered Terry said, "I love you."

"Oh, Sweetie Pie," the female voice replied. "Is you all tucked in bed for nitey-night?"

"Uh huh," Terry acknowledged. "And how's my baby? You all comfy, you little darlin'?"

Josephine held up reasonably well, for she had already experienced many months of marital deterioration. I turned off the tape for a moment and asked her if the woman's voice sounded familiar.

She nodded. "It's a woman from up the street. She runs a restaurant. Terry and I used to eat there all the time."

We listened to the remaining thirty minutes of the tape. The lovey-dovey baby talk never stopped.

"I want a divorce," Josephine said firmly, as the tape ran to the end.

"Well, we've got to find out where and when they meet," I said. I handed her a sixty-minute tape. "Let's try for a longer conversation."

The next tape gave us a full hour of baby talk, but no hint as to the time and place of the rendezvous. So we tried for a third time with another sixty-minute tape.

Josephine brought that cassette back to me along with an explanation. She had been afraid that the recorder was visible through the ventilator grate, she said. So when she installed this tape she had pushed the equipment back into the shaft. She hoped she had not disrupted the machinery.

I assured her that the equipment was tough and played the tape.

"I'm gonna have to spank your cute little bottom," Terry told his lover, never dreaming that his wife would listen to the entire conversation.

"He never talked to me like that," Josephine muttered angrily.

"Spank my bottom," the woman shrieked. "Oooooh, I'd like that!"

"You're a naughty little girl."

"Well, I try to be, Daddy."

This infantile conversation continued for about thirty-five minutes, when even the lovers seemed to be tiring of it. There was a brief silence, and suddenly a strange buzzing sound exploded onto the tape, like nothing I had ever heard before on a telephone tap. A deep, rhythmic, rasping sound—like a tiger roaring spasmodically—continued to the end of the hour-long tape.

Josephine apologized for breaking my equipment, but I reassured her. I couldn't imagine any malfunction in the electronic machinery producing such a sound, and I wondered if another electric device nearby had produced the interference. We drove over to the home and I ripped the bugging equipment out of the wall to check. Everything seemed to be in order.

Yet for a solid week our telephone tap produced no answer to the mystery. We would record roughly a half hour of love talk, and then the recorder would pick up nothing but the ear-splitting buzzing noise.

And at no time did the couple give any clue that would enable us to track them to a love nest. We followed Terry a couple of times that week, but he was apparently leading an innocent life other than his late-night phone conversations.

Josephine suspected that Terry would make his adulterous move when he said he was going to visit his parents over the weekend. We scheduled surveillance on him for the weekend and hoped that the tape would give us some clue as to the couple's destination.

On Thursday morning I removed and examined the equipment once again. Since Terry and his girlfriend never seemed to make any plans at night, I was curious to discover what they said to each other in the morning, before Josephine arrived home from work. Perhaps that was when they set their rendezvous. So I installed a timing device on the recorder that would activate it at 5:30 A.M.—about fifteen minutes before Terry woke up to go to work.

On Friday we were both disappointed to hear the buzzing from the very moment the recording began. Suddenly the tape blared forth an unmistakable sound: Terry's alarm clock was ringing. The buzzing stopped momentarily, started again, then stopped. We heard Terry yawn and turn off the alarm clock. The buzzing was gone.

Finally we understood. The mysterious electronic buzzing was the horrendous sound of a man snoring into a telephone from point-blank range.

"Honey," Terry's voice said softly. "C'mon, honey, wake up."

We heard stirrings on the other end of the line. Then a yawn. "Oooooh. Good morning."

"Did you sleep well?"

"Uh huh. 'Cause you were near."

The lovers then began to baby-talk. Incredibly, they seemed to have formed the habit of sleeping in their separate beds with their telephones linking them together all night. How the woman managed to sleep through Terry's hideous snoring I'll never understand!

Though we solved the mystery of the buzz, we came up with a blank on adultery evidence. From the conversation it was apparent that Terry was going to Pennsylvania that weekend—but he was going alone. His lover complained that she had to work at the restaurant.

I was called away on another case, and it was the following Wednesday before I once again talked to Josephine. She telephoned my office and asked to meet me at the motel. She handed me a brown-paper shopping bag, and I looked inside to find my recorder and telephone tap, its connections obviously ripped violently from the wall.

"I told Terry," she said.

Instinctively I looked around the parking lot to make sure that Terry had not followed her.

"We listened to the tapes together," Josephine continued. "He cried, and said he was sorry."

My client burst into tears. "He said he still loves me," she sobbed.

Once in a while I'm lucky enough to help a couple find a happy ending. Sometimes my investigation forces a man and woman to confront one another openly and honestly for the first time in years. Josephine called me three months later to tell me that I had saved her marriage. She and Terry had fallen back in love. They were sleeping together.

And every night, during her coffee break, she calls her husband.

8

PLAYING POST OFFICE

"I'm taking my clothes off, but I'm not quite bare bottomed."
"Well, I am."
"I'd like to grab a hold of that sweet thing."
"Uh huh. Have a bite ... either end. You can leave your trademark."

One problem with wiretapping is that it produces a record of the conversation that can get into the wrong hands. The statements above are taken from a one-hour discussion between two employees at a branch of the United States Postal Service in Washington, D.C. The first speaker is a black man. The second is a white woman married to an extremely prejudiced man from Tennessee. When the redneck husband was forced to listen to this tape, a routine adultery case nearly turned into murder.

It all began when I was contacted by a Washington divorce attorney and asked to take the case of a man I will call Robert Bryan. I met Robert at the attorney's office and listened to his familiar, sad story. He had been married for twenty-four years. After raising two children to high school age, his wife, Mary, had found a job to keep herself occupied. Robert did not like the fact that she was working at the Post Office, because "too many niggers worked there," he said. Nevertheless, Mary continued at her job.

When she was transferred to the 4 P.M.-to-midnight shift the marriage began to fall apart. It appeared to me to be yet another case in which a woman, having been put into a subordinate role as wife and mother, suddenly rebelled when she discovered other facets of life. Robert seemed the type of man who might be dismally unimaginative as a lover. The fact that Mary had moved to a separate bedroom was a good indication that she had found someone else.

Robert was firm in his resolve to divorce her. The attorney, Evelyn Spencer, was concerned that a casual divorce would hurt Robert financially. The couple owned a nice home and a cabin in the mountains. They had money in the bank.

Evelyn advised her client that an adultery investigation was the best way to safeguard his possessions.

Robert had a more emotional reason for hiring me. He fiercely demanded that I discover why Mary would arrive home at 2 A.M. from her midnight shift, and then receive a long phone call at 2:30!

Robert and Mary were on what I call screaming terms. The only communication between them was at a high-decibel level. Mary never bothered to clean Robert's room, so I felt fairly safe in hiding a recorder inside his cluttered closet. I ran a line to the phone in Mary's room.

Once I had installed the tap I took a special precaution in view of Robert's explosive nature.

"This is a sophisticated piece of equipment," I lied to him. "I need a special recorder to play the tape. If you will drop the tapes off at my office on your way to work in the morning, I'll listen to them and report to you."

My motive, of course, was to prevent the violent reaction that would probably occur if Robert heard what I feared would be on the tapes.

The first words on the first tape made me pretty sure, from the voice's tone and dialect, that the lover was a black man. For nearly an hour he carried on a conversation with Mary that left little doubt that they were enjoying a very active sex life. However, there was no clue as to where and when they met.

Robert called me in the afternoon for a report. I had to inform him that it definitely appeared his wife was committing adultery. I told him it seemed to be a man she knew from work, but we could not yet establish his identity.

On his way to work the next morning Robert dropped off a second tape. It contained more sex talk, and then the man suggested, since he had the day off and would not see her at work, that Mary come over to his house early in the afternoon. She accepted the invitation eagerly. Apparently she never had visited him at his home before, so he gave Mary (and me) detailed directions as to how to find his house. I gulped down a cup of coffee, grabbed Jim Metz, and we immediately placed Mary under surveillance.

She left home around noon, attired in a black-and-white-checked dress. We followed her easily from a distance, since we knew her destination. She parked her car in a residential neighborhood and walked to the door of a two-story brick home. A blue Cadillac with a white vinyl top was parked in the driveway. She was greeted at the door by a tall, slim black man forty to forty-five years of age. He was dressed in dark slacks and a long-sleeved sport shirt striped in red and white. I took notes while Jim shot a few feet of excellent color film.

Unfortunately for our purposes, Mary did not kiss her lover at the door. The lack of any open sign of affection could make this a weak case. Nevertheless we watched the house carefully for two and a half hours. There was no visible activity until Mary came back out the front door, accompanied by the man. He was dressed in the same dark slacks but had only a T-shirt on. Jim documented the occurrence with movie film. A judge would want to know why, when a woman visited a man, the man would remove his outer shirt.

Robert was understandably anxious to learn the results of our surveillance. I was reluctant to tell him. But Evelyn is an aggressive attorney, and she decided to explain the situation to Robert the following afternoon. I was not present at the meeting, but Evelyn told me later it was one of the few times she thought a client was going to slug her. In his fury and frustration Robert did break one of her office chairs with a violent kick.

Evelyn managed to convince Robert that our case was still extremely shaky. We had placed the couple together for several hours, but had little evidence other than the man removing his shirt. (The wiretap discussions could not, of course, be used as evidence.) Evelyn suggested that Robert take the children up to their West Virginia cabin for this coming weekend. This would not only keep him away from Mary but would also give us a chance to catch the lovers.

Robert brought me a tape Friday morning and told me he was going away for the weekend. As an afterthought he remarked that what he *should* do was come home unexpectedly Saturday night and catch Mary with her boyfriend.

By this time we had identified the lover by tracing the license plate of his Cadillac. His name was Tony Jones. He was married, but we had learned from the tapes that his wife had moved out of the house about two weeks prior to our investigation.

The third tape hinted at some sort of on-the-job meeting place. Mary remarked to Tony that sex was even better at his house than it was at work.

I determined to wrap up the case over the weekend. Robert's emotional situation was deteriorating rapidly, and the sooner we could gather enough evidence to force Mary to leave home, the better. By Friday evening Robert was on his way to West Virginia with the children; Mary and Tony were working side by side at the Post Office, and Jim Metz and I were doing our best to find a way to watch them.

The Post Office is a gloomy old structure that hums with twenty-four-hour activity. Each employee must wear an identification badge with his photograph on it. Entrances to the work areas are guarded by unsmiling men in uniform.

Where in this hubbub of activity could they find a place secluded enough to make love? Jim and I first posed as customers, but we had a poor view of the work area. And if we had tried to remain in the lobby from 4 P.M. to midnight we would have been as conspicuous as the wanted posters.

Finally we found a vantage point outside the building near the loading dock, where the big red, white and blue trucks were filled with mail. Hovering around the area as if we belonged there, we managed to keep a pretty good watch on Tony. Mary, however, was nowhere to be seen. Around midnight Tony disappeared from view. As the flood of employees left the office, we tried to spot the couple among them. But we could not find either subject, so we checked the employee parking lot. Both their cars were still there.

Finally, about 2:30 A.M., Mary emerged from a side door near the loading dock and walked to her car. We followed her home and watched the house all night with no luck.

Bleary-eyed, we waited outside in the morning until Mary left the house. Jim followed her to a grocery store while I used her husband's key to sneak into the house and replace the tape. By the time Mary arrived back home, Jack Fogerty had arrived to take over the surveillance with another assistant.

Driving home for some sleep, I played the tape on my car recorder. There was more talk, very sexy and very detailed, about their lovemaking the night before somewhere in the Post Office building. Suddenly the couple started talking about Robert. . . . I screeched to a stop at the first phone booth and called Evelyn.

"Can you get in touch with Robert?" I asked. "Make sure he doesn't try to come home tonight!" Then I told her what Tony had said to Mary.

I was barely asleep when my office called. Robert had insisted on driving back from West Virginia for the day (leaving his children at the cabin). He wanted more details as to why he couldn't come home that night. Evelyn insisted that I bring the tape over to her office.

Everyone has a style of working. I would have burned the tape before I let Robert hear it, but Evelyn believes in shock therapy. She hoped that listening to the tape would convince Robert of the need for us to substantiate the adultery case.

Robert walked into the office dressed in blue jeans. He chain-smoked throughout the meeting, flicking his cigarette ashes onto the carpet. While the three of us listened to the tape, Robert's neck turned redder and redder. Here are a few of the juicier exchanges the poor husband had to hear:

Tony: "My God, you're a sweet hunk of woman ... wild ..."
Mary: "I just need a man ... like you."
Tony: "Yes, darling, like I need a woman like you, you beautiful doll."
Mary: "Ummmm. I'll move over. I'm cold."
Tony: "I'll eat you up ... mmm. Push 'em up against me. I just eat that stuff up."

Tony: "I'll go shave now."
Mary: "Have a bite, love. I'll wait here for you."
Tony: "I'll nip you just a little bit."
Mary: "You better finish, too."
Tony: "Baby, you're some kinda turn-on."

Tony: "I'd like to flip your switch right now."
Mary: "Come on."
Tony: "You know something strange? You turn on quicker that way than the other way. Instant. Yep. That's

your instant turn-on switch. One bite and you're on. That's all it really takes. One nibble. You love it."

Mary: "Mmmmmmmmmmmm."

Tony: "You're my kind of woman. You like everything . . . nothing held back."

Mary: "I'm so happy with you, because we started off right."

Tony: "Nothing held back."

Mary: "Sometimes when I talk to people . . . my life is based on a big lie . . . but I'm so happy and contented with you because I have been truthful with you. I mean it when I say I would do anything for you."

Tony: "You've proved that, darling."

As if this were not enough torture for poor Robert, the lovers then began discussing their mutual problem—him. Tony wondered aloud if he could come sleep with Mary at her house that night, but she was afraid that Robert might come home unexpectedly—to check on her. Listening to that, Robert sat up in surprise. Was she reading his mind?

Then Tony slyly suggested what Mary could do if Robert did come home unexpectedly:

Tony: "You could just shoot through the door."

Mary: "What?"

Tony: "Take your gun and shoot him through the door. Everyone knows he's supposed to be gone all weekend. You could say you thought someone was breaking in."

Mary: "Yeah. I'd be rid of him then."

Evelyn shut off the tape. Robert's body began to shake all over. "I'm going to beat the shit out of them!" he shouted. "I'll kill that bastard!"

Evelyn pulled some Valium pills out of her desk drawer and persuaded Robert to gulp them down. We tried to talk coolly to him until the tranquilizers could take effect. Then I had Jack drive Robert back up to the cabin for Saturday night, leaving him stranded without his own car.

Exhausted but determined, Jim Metz and I played post office once again that night. We caught scattered glimpses of our subjects, but they seemed to avoid each other while working. We watched carefully as the shift changed at midnight, but neither Mary nor Tony left the building.

Mary disappeared. We kept watching Tony from our vantage point near the loading dock, but he seemed to be attending to business. About 12:30 he grabbed a clipboard and walked directly toward us. Caught flatfooted in his path, we couldn't run.

"... So Harry spent all weekend rebuilding the carb and blew the whole goddamn engine last night," I said to Jim.

"Geeez," he replied. "I bet he was sore. He loves that Chevy better than his wife and kids."

"Yeah, well, he has to bury the Chevy now."

Tony walked past us into the rear of a mail truck. He pulled the back door shut and we could hear him tossing mail bags around. We moved closer to the truck and continued our meaningless conversation. Thumping noises came from the truck, then quiet. After a few minutes we thought we heard a giggle.

We moved to a point where we could carefully watch the only exit from the truck, and waited for an hour and a half.

The loading dock was nearly deserted when, around 2 A.M., the back door of the truck swung open and the couple walked out together. Tony kissed her quickly, and they walked to their cars.

Monday morning Evelyn decided to act before Robert's anger resulted in tragedy. By messenger she sent a letter to Mary, informing her that she had been investigated for adultery. She asked Mary to come to her office to discuss the case.

That same afternoon Mary arrived at the attorney's office. As Evelyn had gambled, the woman was too upset and flustered to bring her own lawyer with her, so Evelyn was free to continue her ploy. She snapped a tape cassette into a recorder and allowed Mary to listen to one of her sexy conversations with Tony.

Embarrassed, ashamed and afraid, Mary moved out of the house that very day. A week later Robert's attorney called her and arranged a quiet, out-of-court divorce. Robert paid Mary half the equity in the home, but Mary gave up her share of the household furnishings and the cabin. She asked for no alimony.

About a year later Shirley and I took our children for a Sunday-afternoon drive, and we stopped for a snack at a McDonald's that happened to be near the Post Office. There in the restaurant, nibbling away on their French fries, were Mary and Tony. His hand rested on her arm.

I nudged Shirley and told her who they were. Shirley studied the look in Mary's eyes, then assured me, "She's a happy woman."

9

THE JUDGE AVOIDS
THE JURY

Brewster MacDonald III owned a vacation cottage in
Maine, furnished with priceless early American antiques
and a twenty-two-year-old blonde. Brewster wanted to
marry the girl, but unfortunately that would have made him
a bigamist.

His wife, Marianne, was quite content to occupy Brewster's $200,000 home in one of Washington's most fashiona-
ble neighborhoods. When Brewster moved out he agreed to
pay Marianne temporary support of $1,800 per month.
Later, through his attorney, he asked Marianne for a
divorce, offering to buy her a townhouse and pay her $800
per month alimony. Marianne flatly refused to lower her
standard of living.

That's when Brewster's attorney decided to investigate
Marianne for adultery. Brewster, a cultured, timid-looking
man, probably would have agreed to a more generous
settlement rather than face Marianne's wrath. But the
attorney prodded him into the fight.

The client's inherited wealth made the cost of the
investigation no consideration. The attorney hired not only
me but a second divorce detective as well. I will call him
Sam.

One afternoon during Marianne's weekly appointment
at the hairdresser's three nervous men sneaked up the

driveway of Brewster's former residence. Brewster **led Sam** and me into the attached garage, where we **discovered a** locked file cabinet that contained his tax records. Marianne, he assured us, did not have a key to the file. In the back of one of the drawers we installed a telephone tap, hooked to a recorder. Drilling through the garage wall into the house, we spliced into Marianne's telephone line. After showing Brewster how to retrieve the tape cassettes, we scurried away.

The investigation moved slowly, but Sam and I were not worried. The attorney had instructed us to spend seven days a week on the case until it was ended. We were to be very careful not to alarm Marianne. During the first week Brewster brought us three tapes, which consisted mainly of innocent conversations with the hairdresser, the doctor's office, and Marianne's girlfriends. But, after his third trip back to the garage, Brewster refused to return. He was fearful that his sneaky visits back home would attract the attention of his neighbors. He preferred to spend his time in Maine and leave the dirty work to us.

Neither Sam nor I wished to risk a jail term for breaking and entering, so we were forced to find another means of investigating Marianne's activities. Without Brewster's help we were reluctant to return to the garage to remove the tap, so we just let it sit there.

We persuaded Brewster to order an extension phone for his home number and have it installed in his office. Since Brewster's home phone was still registered in his name, his request was not questioned. The extension was installed while Marianne was out of town, and she didn't realize that Brewster (and two detectives) could sit in his office and record her private telephone conversations.

Unfortunately for Brewster's bank account, Marianne seemed to be behaving herself. She occasionally talked to a male friend, but the conversations appeared to be innocent. A couple of times she made lunch dates with her attorney at one of Washington's fashionable restaurants, and we followed hopefully. The luncheons were long, but the two never showed any public signs of affection.

One evening I was in Brewster's office when the telephone rang. I activated the tape recorder as Marianne answered. The man's voice sounded vaguely familiar, but I couldn't place it. He asked Marianne if he could stop by for a visit.

"Sure," she replied. "I'll start a fire burning in the fireplace. It'll be cozy."

"Sounds nice," the man replied. "I'd like to see your bearskin rug."

While this was hardly convincing evidence of adultery, it was the first time a lone male was coming to visit Marianne. I placed the recorder on automatic to document any further calls, alerted Sam to join me, and headed for Marianne's house.

In a few minutes a big black car pulled up in front of the house. A distinguished-looking man in a dark suit emerged and walked toward the door.

"Son of a bitch!" I muttered in amazement. Sam stared also. We both knew the man, for we had testified many times in his courtroom. He was a respected judge in one of the jurisdictions in the Washington metropolitan area. We ducked low, for he would recognize us on sight.

His Honor remained inside the house for about two hours but, unfortunately for our purposes, gave us no evidence of dishonorable conduct. The lights remained on. A patrolling police cruiser kept us from moving closer to the house.

Nevertheless we had our first speck of mildly incriminating evidence against Marianne, and the attorney was pleased that we had managed to involve a prominent person. We had little doubt that the judge would try to suppress our evidence before it could appear in open court.

The scene repeated itself many times over the next few weeks. The judge, a married man, would call our subject in the early evening. The two would chat for a few moments, and there was always just a hint of spice in the conversation. Many times Marianne joked that they had to be careful of their words, because the phone might be tapped. After each call we placed the house under surveillance and documented the judge's arrival. He never stayed more than two hours. They never turned out the lights. They never showed any public signs of affection.

The relationship could have been innocent, but I'm sure the judge would never have wanted his wife to know of the visits. While we could not prove adultery, we were accumulating some embarrassing evidence that might be enough to persuade Marianne to settle out of court.

Then, as often happens, the client decided to complicate our job. Brewster stopped by the house one Friday night to deliver an alimony check before leaving for a weekend in Maine. While he was there he apparently made a caustic remark to Marianne about the judge. Then he split, leaving Sam and me behind to take the heat for his blunder. Marianne was determined to find out how he had learned about her boyfriend.

Early Saturday morning I was in Brewster's office when Marianne called the Chesapeake and Potomac Telephone Company. "I believe that my telephone line may be tapped," she told the service representative, as I nearly dropped the extension phone to the floor. The telephone company agreed to send someone over to investigate.

I hurriedly called Sam, and he joined me in Brewster's office. We spent the morning frantically trying to remember if we had wiped our fingerprints off the equipment in the garage file cabinet.

Around noon we monitored a call that Marianne made to her attorney at his home. She furiously told him that the phone company had discovered a telephone tap in Brewster's file cabinet. She knew that Brewster did not have the courage to install the equipment himself, so she suspected that he had hired a detective.

"I want to sue that detective for every penny he's got!" she told her attorney and two squirming detectives. "I'll be in your office first thing Monday morning to draw up the papers."

Marianne slammed the phone down and began to dial another number. Suddenly Brewster's office phone rang in my ear. Marianne let it ring about twenty times before she gave up. During the next hour she dialed her husband's office at least a dozen times.

While I continued to monitor her line, Sam got on another phone to try to reach Brewster in Maine. He had no luck. Brewster's attorney was also unreachable. Sam and I were sitting on the hot seat alone.

Finally Marianne placed another call, and I recognized the voice that I knew so well from the courtroom. He stammered and stuttered for a moment when Marianne told him about the tap.

"You ... you mean ... all our conversations ... were taped?" he asked.

Marianne's reply was embellished with profanity.

The judge let out a long sigh. "Listen ... are you going to be home tonight? I'd like to come over and discuss this whole thing with you."

"Sure," Marianne replied. "I need some advice."

They talked for a few more moments as the judge tried to calm her. Finally she said, "I wish I could find Brewster. I'm sure he's working in his office, but he won't answer the phone." Then she said determinedly, "I'm going over there and make him give me the name of the detective."

She slammed the phone down, and I shouted at Sam, "She's coming here! You get the recorder. I'll work on the lock."

It takes about twenty-five minutes to drive from Brewster's home to his office. During that time Sam and I set a new speed record for covering up evidence. While Sam cleared the recording equipment out of the office and stashed it in his car, I ran down to the street and rummaged through the trunk of my car for a lock that resembled the one on Brewster's office door. Frantically I ripped out the old lock and installed the new one. As a final precaution we even removed the tag from the face of the extension phone that showed it was listed in Marianne's home number.

The office was small and offered little refuge. Our hearts pounding, we slid under a couple of desks as the elevator door opened. We could see a woman's figure through the frosted glass doors of Brewster's office.

A key clicked into the lock and attempted to turn. It rattled back and forth as the frustrated woman realized that the lock had been changed. She kicked the door in anger and marched away.

Sam and I looked at each other and breathed again. We waited a full ten minutes before retrieving the recorder and hooking it back up to Marianne's phone.

That evening his honor arrived at Marianne's home promptly at seven in an attempt to save his marriage and career. He stayed longer than usual, undoubtedly resorting to every form of persuasion his legal mind could conjure up. When he finally left around midnight he appeared tired and upset. He nearly pulled his car out in front of a police cruiser.

We were most anxious to hear what Marianne had to say the next day. She called a girlfriend and had a long, angry discussion about the wiretap. We were thankful to hear her say that "friends" had persuaded her not to prosecute. A court case would be too embarrassing, she said.

The next three weeks brought the two rival attorneys together for many negotiating sessions. Brewster's attorney had the advantage, however, because two private detectives were listening to all of Marianne's phone calls concerning the case. She never dreamed that we had tapped her phone twice!

Brewster's attorney stood firm for the original offer of a townhouse and $800 a month. Marianne's attorney argued loud and hard, but we were well aware that Marianne had decided not to go to court.

Eventually Marianne accepted the **settlement**. Brewster paid $60,000 for a fashionable townhouse. Marianne lives there comfortably, but quite a step down from her previous style.

Except for Marianne, everyone was quite happy with the settlement. Brewster married his sweetheart in Maine. The attorneys pocketed handsome fees. The judge avoided the jury.

And Sam and I stayed out of jail.

10

SEX IN STEREO

On a Thursday evening a few years ago residents of a middle-class apartment complex in the Virginia suburbs of Washington were treated to a radio first. Those who were tuned to the frequency of one of the city's most popular FM stereo stations heard a new release entitled "Fuck Me, Fuck Me, Fuck Me," sung by Melinda Rogers and the Squeaky Bedsprings.

One of the fascinated radio listeners was Melinda's husband.

The story of this broadcasting breakthrough began at an attorney's office, where I was called in to handle the divorce investigation for a local policeman. When Arnie Rogers broke up with his wife, Melinda, he only wanted to take three items with him—the children. Melinda, of course, refused. Arnie's attorney believed there was a chance to win custody, because Melinda had already begun to date other men. Arnie assured us that his wife's sex drive was strong enough to make her an adulteress.

Both the attorney and I advised Arnie that he must keep his own zipper up until the custody issue was settled. He agreed. He told us he was living with a friend from the police force.

Melinda went out every Tuesday and Thursday night with her girlfriend Glenda. Together the two would barhop around the sleazy Fourteenth Street area of Washington. They had little difficulty finding friends, for Glenda was a striking woman with beautiful blond hair. Melinda, with dark hair and a somewhat tacky appearance, did all right herself.

So it was that Guy Morgan and I were sitting downtown in Benny's Rebel Room on a Tuesday evening, watching the two women from across the crowded, raucous joint. The place was like a supermarket for sex, and the girls displayed themselves as though they were a selection of choice meats. I recognized one or two of them as prostitutes, but most of the girls seemed merely out for some free fun.

And that was in good supply. Melinda and Glenda danced till midnight, but despite a lot of flirting, they were alone when we followed them out to the street.

I sent Guy to get our car while I followed our subjects up Fourteenth Street to I Street. They turned a corner, and suddenly I heard giggles. I spotted the two women flirting with a couple of motorcycle policemen from the District of Columbia force.

They were too far away for me to understand the conversation, but there were plenty of laughs. I leaned casually against the building for about ten minutes, studying the window of an establishment that called itself "The Largest Adult Bookstore in the World." Finally the motorcycles roared to life, and the two policemen sped down Fourteenth Street.

The girls walked quickly to a parking lot, and I hopped into our surveillance car with Guy. Instead of heading straight home, Melinda turned her car back toward Fourteenth Street. There, circling and horsing around in the middle of the pavement, were the two motorcycle policemen. When they saw Melinda and Glenda they waved, turned away, and drove south. At E Street they turned left as though headed for the precinct headquarters. The women followed.

The streets in that section of town are virtually deserted late at night, and we could not afford to give away our presence.

"Pull over to F Street," I told Guy.

We glided along carefully, watching from the parallel street. At each intersection we could look to the right and catch a glimpse of our subjects. But at Sixth Street there was no sign of life. Guy pulled the car quickly down the block to the right, but E Street was deserted.

"They've got to be here somewhere," I muttered.

We searched several blocks. We even checked the parking lot at precinct headquarters. There was no sign of Melinda's car or the motorcycles.

Back at Sixth and E we looked carefully around the area. The foursome had to be somewhere nearby.

The parking ramp! The multi-story parking lot was the only hiding place on the block.

We jumped from the car and ran toward the ramp. But as I leaped over a cement barricade a bright light hit me and a deep voice boomed, "What the hell are you doing?"

I calmed down after I recognized the face of a police lieutenant I had known for several years. I knew I could trust this particular lieutenant, so I leveled with him. I told him we were following the wife of a policeman from Virginia.We suspected that she and another woman were inside the parking lot with two uniformed motorcycle cops.

The lieutenant looked shocked. "Stay here," he commanded. "I'll check it out for you."

He drove his cruiser slowly up the ramp, the searchlight peering into every corner. The car disappeared, and we waited ten minutes in the early-morning silence. Quietly the car reappeared and the lieutenant drove over to us.

"Nobody's up there," he informed us. He watched us drive away and headed his own car toward the precinct.

We turned the corner.

"Stop," I said to Guy.

"Why?"

Intuition? Detective's nose? "I just have a feeling."

Moving on foot through the shadows next to the

buildings, we crept back toward the intersection and squatted behind a brick wall. My eyes were riveted on the entrance to the parking ramp.

Five minutes passed. My bones began to ache.

"They're not here," Guy whispered.

"Shhhhh!"

Five more minutes. I was ready to leave but my hunch wouldn't let me.

Va-roooom! the roar from the top level of the parking garage shattered the stillness.

Va-roooom! a second cycle gunned to life.

Two noisy machines burst onto the street, piloted by a pair of grim-faced policemen. They roared past our hiding place and headed for the precinct headquarters.

Another five minutes. Melinda's car crept from the garage, tucked its tailpipe between its legs and scurried for Virginia, while I cussed out my friend, the lieutenant.

The case was blown. There seemed no way we could catch Melinda once she knew of our investigation. I met with Arnie the next afternoon to inform him of the lieutenant's dirty trick. Enraged, he insisted that I report the matter officially to the District of Columbia police department so that the two motorcycle policemen and the lieutenant would be disciplined. The more I thought about it, the better it sounded.

I called the lieutenant's immediate superior—a captain whom I had also known for years. Angrily I told him the story and he sympathized with me. He promised to have the lieutenant call me.

When my ex-friend phoned, I was mad and I told him so.

Meekly he apologized.

"I don't want your damn apology," I told him. "All I want is the truth, and if I find out you're bullshitting me I'm going to subpoena you and your two buddies on an adultery charge. I want to know what you told them, and I want to know how much those women heard."

He swore that he had only spoken to the cops, that he had not blown the case for me.

Naturally I didn't believe a word he said.

"Let's hold off for two or three weeks," I told Arnie. "Maybe by that time Melinda will become bold once again."

Arnie thought it over carefully. He had a rather peculiar relationship with his estranged wife. The two of them hated each other, but they also talked on the phone every morning. Arnie reasoned that Melinda would have cursed him out that very morning if she had known of my investigation.

"I think you should continue the case," he said. "She's going out tomorrow night. And I'm in a hurry to get this over with."

"Why?"

"Well ..."

Then Arnie's story poured out. He was in love with another woman. In fact, he had been living with her since he moved away from Melinda. His address with his police buddy was merely a front.

"I gotta catch her before she catches me," he said.

I took a deep breath. This case was getting more troublesome all the time. Arnie and I discussed how we could wrap it up quickly.

"It would really help," I said slowly, "if we could listen in on Melinda's conversations with Glenda." The two women spent a lot of time together in Melinda's apartment.

Arnie was in full uniform the next morning when we drove up to his old apartment. We watched Melinda walk to her car and drive away. She had told Arnie she was going shopping all morning. Arnie led me up to the apartment and unlocked the door with his key.

Quickly we moved to the bedroom of the rectangular

apartment. I took an FM transmitter and screwed it into place behind the headboard of the bed. The little bug is only about two and a half by four inches, but its powerful signal can be picked up for nearly a mile. I ran an antenna wire the length of the headboard and set the frequency. With the turn of a screw the broadcasting frequency can be set at any FM signal. To avoid detection I always set the frequency as far as possible away from any local FM station, so that the neighbors do not tune in on the bugged conversation.

I was turning the screw when Arnie hollered at me.

"She's coming back!" he shouted, staring down into the parking lot.

We scrambled for our tools and hurried out the back hallway as Melinda returned to her apartment. But the job was completed. We would be able to hear every word of conversation inside the apartment for the next thirty hours, until the batteries wore down.

Guy and I began surveillance at 4 P.M. that same day. I switched on the FM receiver designed to pick up the bug, and immediately heard Melinda cussing out her children. The bug was working fine.

Hours later Melinda took the children to a babysitter, met Glenda and headed downtown for Benny's Rebel Room. This time they singled out two sailors for their attention.

About 1 A.M. Guy and I watched Melinda and Glenda lead two sailors to her car. The frolicsome foursome headed for Virginia. One of the sailors was driving drunkenly, and we felt safe in following close. I turned on my car radio to my favorite FM station.

When they reached Melinda's apartment, Glenda drove off in her own car with one of the sailors. Guy went to tape the door while I drove up a hill to a parking lot that afforded an excellent view of the apartment. I switched on the special FM receiver in time to hear Melinda invite her sailor inside. But the conversation was strangely full of echoes.

I switched off the special receiver and realized that the bug was transmitting on the same frequency as my favorite station. For many blocks around the apartment it would completely drown out the normal signal. I could only hope that anyone listening in would be too fascinated to complain.

Melinda and the sailor provided some of the most innovative radio programming in history. Guy joined me in my car and together we listened to drunken small talk. The conversation quickly moved into the bedroom.

We heard shoes drop to the floor and were so captivated by these intriguing sounds of preparation that we failed to see the police car pull up behind us.

"Anything happening?" Arnie asked. "I was on patrol nearby so I thought I'd check with you." Suddenly he heard his wife squeal, and he jumped into the back seat to listen.

Someone should invent oil to prevent bedsprings from squeaking. They never fail to indicate the exact nature of the activity taking place above them. As the springs squeaked rhythmically Arnie grew silent. Guy and I held our breath, for Arnie's service revolver was, of course, strapped to his belt.

Melinda moaned.

The sailor groaned.

Melinda shouted, "Fuck me, fuck me, fuck me" to her radio fans.

"That's not her!" Arnie whispered. "She never said that to me. That must be Glenda."

Once more Melinda shouted, and this time Arnie knew for sure. He grabbed for the door handle. "I'm gonna go up there and shoot them both." he yelled.

Guy and I reminded Arnie that murder, not to mention bugging, is looked upon with disfavor in Virginia. If he wanted the stupid satisfaction of killing his wife instead of divorcing her, he would pay for it with a life sentence.

Finally he calmed down. So did the apartment. But after twenty minutes it began all over again. The springs squeaked louder and louder.

Now Arnie took it differently. Once he accepted the fact of Melinda's adultery, he seemed fascinated.

Soon Arnie left in his police car. The sailor left by cab.

The case was a prime example of how the average attorney screws up a divorce hearing. Melinda's hot-shot young lawyer was not about to share his fee with a private detective, and his greediness saved Arnie's neck. Any bumbling detective would quickly have discovered that Arnie was living with another woman, but Melinda's lawyer remained unaware of the affair. When all the testimony had been heard, Arnie appeared to be pure and wholesome compared to his frolicsome wife, who barhopped in downtown Washington and then entertained sailors in her darkened apartment.

The judge decided that Benny's Rebel Room was not a wholesome environment for a mother. He awarded custody to Arnie, while Melinda burst into tears and her lawyer's mouth dropped open.

Arnie married his girlfriend and together they are raising the kids.

He called me a few months later to thank me for my work. Then, to my surprise, he asked for a job—he was intrigued by the life style of a divorce detective. I politely refused, remembering his unprofessional display of temper. He soon quit the police force anyway, moved to New Jersey, and opened up his own detective agency.

Before long, our paths were destined to cross once more.

11

MOTORCYCLE MANIAC

Gloria Schultz was paying the monthly bills. She was sure there should be more money in the checking account, so she searched back through the stubs. To her surprise she discovered an $800 payment to a private detective named Arnie Rogers—my old client.

She stormed into her husband's office. "What is this?" she demanded.

Mark grinned. "I had you followed," he said. "I know all about your boyfriend."

Gloria, fed up with Mark's wild carousing, had chased him out of the house six months earlier. Though he had been unfaithful for years, Gloria's affair was her first.

"It's not fair," Gloria complained to me later. "He's the sex maniac. Why should I be the one who gets caught?"

She had called me all the way from New Jersey, for I had once handled a case in Washington for one of her close friends. My first task was to find out how much of a case Arnie had compiled, so I dropped by his office in Newark, lied that I had a case in New York, and asked him how his new business was doing. We adjourned to a local bar to talk shop.

Arnie chattered enthusiastically about successes he had had on his early cases, but he complained about his current investigation. The woman, he said, was obviously having an affair, but she was discreet. They always kept the lights on inside the house, and they never showed any public signs of affection. Still, Arnie believed he would have sufficient evidence after one or two more nights of surveillance.

After advising Gloria to behave herself until we caught Mark, I went to work on the case.

Gloria and Mark Schultz owned a large motorcycle dealership. Splitting their marriage had been easy, but the business relationship presented a problem. Mark was a compulsive spender, always in need of cash. Yet he could not drain the business with Gloria watching the books, and he did not want to pay a fair price for her half of the stock. He obviously hoped to make a better settlement by divorcing Gloria on grounds of adultery.

Mark had rented a luxurious house near Newark, complete with a large pool and patio area. I decided I should study the layout of the house from the inside, so Gloria took a close friend into her confidence. Though he had known both of the Schultzes for years, he sympathized with Gloria and agreed to help. One Saturday afternoon the friend dropped by to see Mark and introduced me as a buddy from work. Mark offered us a beer and showed us around the house. While he chatted with his "friend," I was able to spot a good hiding place in a grove of trees near the pool.

But the investigation soon became complicated. To trim his expenses Mark rented out rooms to three other men. The place was constantly occupied by an assortment of people, and it became impossible to prove that any two of them slept together. The four men threw a loud party one weekend, during which we observed Mark hugging several different women while swimming in the pool. Unfortunately, a wet hug is not grounds for divorce in New Jersey.

Weeks passed as we tried in vain to document his adulterous activities. We could not prove anything at home, and we could not follow him on the road, for he had an unfair advantage—a fast Kawasaki cycle. In town he could pass on the right, and ease through stalled traffic. Out on the highway he zoomed along at seventy-five and eighty miles an hour. Surveillance was impossible.

Our chance to catch Mark with his pants down finally came when he told Gloria he was planning to attend a motorcycle dealers' convention at Disney World in Orlando, Florida. He said he was leaving on a Sunday and would be gone for a full week. The shop manager was going with him. Gloria checked the shop manager's work schedule and noted that *he* was not leaving until Wednesday.

Jim Metz and I staked out the house on Saturday evening. Mark took a dip in his pool and then disappeared inside. We watched the house all night.

In the small hours of the morning a green van drove up. The driver rang the doorbell, and in a moment Mark came out. Together the two men wheeled a pair of motorcycles from the garage and loaded them into the back of the van. The stranger then drove away in Mark's car, leaving the van in front of the house.

A half hour later a red Mustang pulled up. A girl got out from the passenger side, and the car sped off. In the darkness we could not get a good view of her, but she appeared to be rather young—certainly much younger than Mark's thirty-six years. The girl knocked on the door and went inside.

Just at daybreak Mark walked out to the van with a couple of suitcases. Then he and the girl carried out that most incriminating bit of evidence—a mattress. They both hopped into the van and the chase was on.

We followed them down the Jersey Turnpike, across the Delaware Memorial Bridge, south on Interstate 95 through Delaware and Maryland, and around Washington into

Virginia. Every hour or so they stopped to change drivers. Every half hour or so Jim and I exchanged the positions of our surveillance cars.

All day long the chase continued through Virginia, the Carolinas and Georgia. Late that night, exhausted, we crossed the state line into Florida.

Surveillance was getting very difficult in the light traffic. Afraid of alarming our subjects, I dropped way behind, barely keeping the van in view.

We lost them as they entered Jacksonville. Frantically we drove through the city checking motel parking lots—but the van had disappeared. Temporarily defeated and disgusted, we rented a room and sank into dreamless sleep.

Over breakfast the next morning we attempted to guess where they might be. They were due in Orlando on Wednesday, but this was only Monday morning. We studied the map. Nearby was a cutoff for Daytona Beach. Since the place is popular with a young crowd, we decided to try there.

In midafternoon we found the van parked along the ocean front. The cycles were gone, giving us time to plan our strategy. If our subjects were going to ride around Daytona Beach, the best way to keep track would be from the seat of another cycle. While Jim kept the van under surveillance I rented some wheels. It was the first time I had ridden a big bike, and the local dealer had to give me instructions.

Disguised in bathing suit, helmet and goggles, I drove off in search of our subjects. In a few minutes I spotted two cycles parked in front of a hamburger stand. Mark was inside, but the girl was standing next to her bike. I pulled into the lot and waved a fellow biker's greeting. She smiled and waved back. I was surprised to see the glint of wire in her mouth—she was still in braces!

Suddenly Mark walked toward us and I drove off. I had shared his beer a few weeks earlier and I didn't care to be remembered. As I drove past he gave me a "Where have I seen you before?" stare.

When they returned from their ride they lay on the mattress in the back of the van and kissed leisurely. Jim preserved the moment on film. Then they walked on the boardwalk. I struck up a friendly conversation with a local policeman, mentioned that I was on surveillance, and he wished me luck.

About midnight the couple returned, climbed into the van, and headed for a nearby motel. But Mark had no intention of paying for a room. They merely hopped out of the van in their bathing suits and went for a swim in the darkened pool. While Jim watched them, I hunted for my new friend, the local policeman. I explained that I needed to identify the girl who was with our subject. He agreed to make a "routine check" for me, and approached the couple as they returned to the van from the pool. Thanks to him we learned that the girl was Annie Davis of Newark. According to her driver's license she was seventeen years old.

After the policeman left, Mark and Annie climbed onto their mattress and shut the back door of the van.

As soon as the windows fogged up we crept close. We watched as the van began to rock back and forth, and before long we heard the familiar moans and groans.

Mark and Annie spent most of Tuesday at the motel pool. While I stood guard, Jim crawled under the van and installed a bumper beeper. Peering inside, he noticed several "roaches"—the telltale butts of marijuana cig-arettes—on the floor.

Late in the afternoon our subjects rode off on their cycles, and I followed carefully on mine. After an hour or so I was hot and sweaty, covered with sand and suntan lotion, so I parked my cycle near the boardwalk, took off my helmet and sunglasses, and hopped under one of the sidewalk showers.

Suddenly Mark joined me!

"Gee, this feels terrific!" he yelled into my ear.

I grunted an unintelligible answer, turned my back on him and walked away as fast as I could. Trying to appear casual, I hopped onto my cycle and kicked the starter. Nothing happened. I kicked it again, but the cycle was dead. I risked a look over my shoulder and saw Mark walking toward me. The obstinate cycle would not start.

Finally I pushed it, almost ran with it. After a block I looked back and saw Mark staring at me, hands on his hips. Then I noticed that I had not turned the ignition switch on. Sheepishly I started the cycle and drove off, certain that I had blown the case.

Despite his obvious suspicions, Mark continued his blatant adultery with the girl. I suppose he was just having too much fun to quit.

On Wednesday morning they both headed for a bath house on the boardwalk. Mark entered the men's side, but Annie saw me taking photos in her direction. She started walking toward me, and I headed for my cycle. From another vantage point Jim witnessed the drama. He had no way of warning me that Mark had emerged from the other side of the bath house, ducked underneath the boardwalk, and was running to intercept me from behind.

When I hopped onto the cycle—this time remembering the ignition switch—I drove away from Annie, right past Mark's nose. Jim told me later that Mark stared after me until I was out of sight.

Mark and Annie packed up. Rational people would have driven home, but our subjects either felt they could lose me, or they just said the hell with it. At any rate, they drove to Disney World in Orlando. Since we could follow them electronically, and since we knew their destination anyway, we could follow easily while remaining out of sight.

My usefulness on the case was largely over, so we set the stage for Jim to conduct an intimate surveillance. Jim located the headquarters booth for the motorcycle convention and registered as a delegate, giving the name of a fictitious dealer from Ithaca, New York. Meanwhile, I made a call to my assistant Linda Goodwin, in Washington, and the trap was set. We got some sleep in preparation for the long night ahead.

Linda's plane arrived in Orlando at 6:30, and Jim met her at the airport while I was out buying a sexy cocktail dress in Linda's size. She changed into it in the hotel room that the three of us would share for the remainder of the week.

I was forced to cool my heels while Jim and Linda attended the opening reception of the convention. They circulated casually among the guests in the hotel meeting room, and as they stood close to Mark and his girlfriend, who were sipping the complimentary champagne, they dangled the bait. They both agreed that their Ithaca business was going so well they should invest some of the profits in a second dealership somewhere else.

"Hi, I'm Mark Schultz," a friendly voice boomed. "This is my wife, Annie." Jim introduced himself and his wife, Linda.

Throughout the evening Mark was careful to stay close to them, and dropped several hints that he was looking for a new partner. Jim encouraged the talk, but then shut it off when the talk got too technical.

"Let's talk business later," he said. "I'm here to have some fun."

"*Smile!*" a voice commanded. Before Mark could object, a flashbulb popped in his face as the convention photographer snapped a photo of the foursome. In the photographer's pocket was a $20 bill and my address.

"You wanna have some fun?" Annie asked. She lowered her voice. "Wanna smoke some grass?"

"Sure."

The four of them left the party and headed for Mark's hotel room. Annie pulled out a plastic bag stuffed with marijuana and rolled several joints. For several hours they partied, laughing and joking together. Linda and Jim steered the conversation to more intimate subjects.

"Want to hear a secret?" Jim teased.

"Sure," Annie said.

"Linda's not my wife. My wife is sitting at home with our four kids. She's my secretary," he said, patting Linda on the behind.

Annie giggled. Mark laughed out loud.

"My wife is home with our two kids," Mark confessed.

Once again Annie giggled through her braces. "Wanna hear something *really* secret?"

Jim and Linda could hardly wait.

"I'm skipping class from high school. My home-room teacher thinks I'm in California with my parents, and my parents think I'm in Pennsylvania with my girlfriend!"

The two detectives and the two subjects remained close during the entire convention. Annie and Linda did some shopping, and Linda learned that the sales manager would drive the van home. Mark and Annie were flying.

While all of this was going on I learned that the only disguise available in Orlando is a pair of mouse ears. Reluctantly I confined my activities to checking the telltale tape on our subjects' hotel-room door.

Sunday I took an early flight to Newark. When the adulterers stepped off the plane in Newark, I was there to snap photos.

It was all over but the shouting, which began a few weeks later when Mark and Annie were served with court papers. Mark shouted obscenities. Annie's parents shouted "statutory rape." But they all shouted out of court, for when Mark's attorney listened to my pretrial deposition, his face went white. My old client Arnie had done a moderately good job of investigating my new client Gloria. But his reports were bland compared to the documentation of Mark's exploits with booze, pot and teenage sex.

So Mark made a private settlement with Annie's parents—I never learned the details. He was forced to sell a majority interest in the motorcycle dealership in order to pay the huge cash settlement negotiated by Gloria's attorney.

He called my Alexandria, Virginia, telephone later and left a very unfriendly message on my tape recorder.

I have never bothered to return the call.

12

FAMILY AFFAIR

Jimmy Lincoln kissed his wife goodbye and drove away from his modest home near Annapolis, Maryland. He put in a long, hard day as a plumber. Before returning home that evening, he stopped at a gymnasium to work out in preparation for an amateur swimming meet. A star swimmer ever since his days in junior high, Jimmy had accumulated an impressive assortment of trophies and medals.

It was 9:30 by the time Jimmy finally arrived home and received the biggest shock of his life. For when he opened the door he found—almost nothing. His trophies and medals were there, along with his clothes, a cot and a few kitchen utensils. But all his home furnishings were gone! So was his wife, Sue. And so were the two little daughters whom Jimmy loved with all his heart.

As he did during any crisis, Jimmy immediately consulted his family. His parents were just as amazed as he was. They came right over to help Jimmy figure out the mystery. His sister Amy and her husband Jack also were puzzled and upset, and they too rushed over to offer consolation.

There were no clues. As far as Jimmy knew, Sue had always been a faithful and loving wife. She sometimes complained that he spent too much time at the swim club, but otherwise she knew him to be a loyal, hard-working, loving husband. The soft-spoken Jimmy collapsed into tears while discussing the situation with his close-knit family.

They called the police, but the disappearance of all the furnishings and clothing proved that the wife had left voluntarily. This was clearly a domestic squabble, not a criminal act. The police could do nothing.

Jimmy called an attorney.

I'll call this lawyer George. He is one of the top five divorce and child-custody specialists in the country. But he could do nothing until Sue and the children were located.

So Jimmy wound up in my office the next day, pouring out his puzzling story to me.

We spent several hours talking that morning. I always try to probe deeply into a client's domestic situation—such a conversation can disclose clues that the client cannot see by himself. I asked Jimmy about Sue's friends and relatives, about her activities during the day, about their sex life. The story that emerged seemed bland, and it occurred to me that perhaps Sue was running away from the boredom of an otherwise good, quiet, simple marriage. Jimmy is a great guy—I got to know him well during the next five months— but he is unimaginative. I wondered if Sue got fed up with the routine.

In his heart Jimmy knew the marriage was ended, for Sue must be completely out of love with him to abandon him. He could never trust her again. But he was desperate to see his children. What, he asked, were the chances of his getting custody of them?

The chances were slim. Custody for a father is a difficult task at best, and in this case the children were two small daughters. It is much easier for a father to win custody of sons. It would take a heap of blatant adultery evidence for a judge to award Jimmy custody of the girls.

Nevertheless, he wanted to try. Amy and Jack gave him much-needed moral support. The parents promised Jimmy they would lend him all the money he needed. It was a substantial promise, for this intricate investigation was destined to last five months and cost more than $6,000.

Over the next few weeks we conducted stakeouts at the homes of Sue's friends. No matter how slight the acquaintance—no matter how much Jimmy assured us that Sue would not be found at the home of any particular person— we checked them all out thoroughly. Sue had simply left no trail.

Three weeks and many dollars later, I asked Jimmy to come in for another talk. He was haggard and pale. He had not been sleeping well; he had not been working out at the gym. The disappearance of his family was destroying him.

"Look, Jimmy," I said, "Sue *did* leave us a clue."

He sat straight up. "What?" he demanded.

"I don't know. It's there. We just haven't found it yet."

We went over and over and over the same questions. The story of Jimmy's marriage was always the same: he had no reason to suspect Sue of adultery.

"Try once more," I said. "Are you *sure* there was nothing suspicious?"

Jimmy was sobbing. "Well ..." he finally said, "there was this thing once. ..."

"What thing once?"

"Well ... I came home one day a little early. Jack was there ... he used to come over a lot. I think someone had been there with Sue when Jack and I suddenly surprised them. Sue seemed very nervous. Well, later I ... I found her panties stuffed behind the sofa."

"How long had Jack been there before you arrived?"

"I dunno. A couple of minutes. I guess her lover scrambled out the back door when Jack drove in the driveway."

I wanted to get mad, but the poor man was suffering too

much. "Jimmy, look at the facts. You came home unexpectedly. Jack was there. Sue was nervous. Later you found her panties in the sofa."

Jimmy looked horrified. "No." He shook his head violently. "No!"

"Jimmy," I said, "do you think Jack might know where Sue is?"

"Oh no. I've already asked him."

Despite Jimmy's reluctance to suspect someone from the family, the hidden panties were an undeniable clue. And it was a frightening one. For the past few weeks Jack had been involved in all the family consultations. It had not seemed necessary for Jimmy to keep the investigation a secret from his very own family! Jack had never actually met me, but he was well aware that I had been hired to find Sue. If he was spying for his sister-in-law the case was going to be very sticky.

I told Jimmy I was going to place Jack under surveillance. And I warned him not to tell anyone—not his sister Amy, not his parents, not his lawyer. He agreed.

Jack is a burly construction worker, helping to build Washington's new Metro subway system, and we staked him out on the job Friday afternoon.

Our first surveillance was short and sour. Jack left work about 4 P.M. and quickly disappeared amid the horrendous Friday-afternoon rush-hour traffic in downtown Washington.

Saturday morning we tried again. Guy Morgan and I sat outside of Jack's home in two separate cars. We could see Amy hanging clothes out to dry in the back yard. Jack left the house around noon, and I followed him easily for about eight blocks while Guy drove on ahead. When I got stuck at a traffic light, I radioed to Guy.

"He's coming your way. Pick him up," I said.

But Jack never arrived where Guy was waiting. The two-block area where he disappeared was the center of a large shopping mall. Several side streets ran off of it, and it was impossible to locate Jack's car. He arrived back home at 3:30.

Sunday he again left home around noon. This time Guy drove ahead to wait at the shopping center. I was tailing Jack as he drove past a large Methodist church, when a policeman suddenly appeared in the road and stopped traffic for a line of churchgoers crossing the street. Frustrated, I pulled past two cars on the right, turned my blinking grille lights on and tapped my siren. The traffic cop looked around, saw that I was driving a car identical to the unmarked patrol cars of the county police, and waved me through.

Guy and I both watched Jimmy's brother-in-law pull into the shopping center and drive behind a cluster of stores. At the end of the huge parking lot he pulled into an alleyway leading to a complex of old apartments. He got out of the car and looked all around him.

"Stay loose," I said to Guy over the radio. "Let's not alarm the son of a bitch now."

Jack took several minutes to assure himself that he was alone. Then drove into the apartment complex.

Twenty minues later we found his car. We waited.

It was a long, sultry June afternoon, and we sweated it out nervously. Nothing happened until about 6:30 in the evening, when we spotted Jack walking between two apartment buildings to his car. He drove home.

Now we had a ray of hope. Jack was visiting someone and I believed it was Sue. Poor Jimmy was dying for news of his children, but I dared not tell him I thought we were close. Now that he was living alone he spent a lot of time at Amy and Jack's house, and we could not afford to have him alert his brother-in-law.

We waited for Jack at the shopping center several evenings the next week. He always parked in a different location near the apartments, and he went to great lengths to disguise his destination.

On Monday we watched as he walked between two buildings and then entered the rear door of another one. As quickly as we could, we followed him inside and taped the doors of all four apartments. Children ran in and out of the building frequently during the summer evening, and our matchsticks littered the hall floors as we tried to keep the doors taped. But, as night settled down, so did the kids, and we were sure that Jack was still somewhere inside.

At 10:30 I checked the doors and all four were properly taped. Fifteen minues later, when Jack emerged from the back door of the building, we knew we had cornered our quarry. Quickly I hustled in and checked the tapes. All four were still intact! Not one of the four doors had been opened!

We had underestimated Jimmy's brother-in-law. We had watched him go in through the back door, but we didn't suspect he was going right out again through the front door. Now we realized that he must have gone to one of the three buildings across from the decoy.

Two nights later I followed him to a grocery store in the shopping center. I went inside and watched him buy a heavy bag of groceries and a six-pack of beer. Then he drove toward the apartment complex.

Guy was waiting near the three buildings we had targeted.

"Guy." I yelled into my car radio. "Get your ass into those buildings and tape the doors. He's headed your way."

Guy had just finished the job and was walking out of the third building when he met Jack coming in the front. While pausing on the landing to tie his shoe, Guy watched Jack unlock the door to apartment number 4.

We pulled our cars to the parking lot behind the building, where we had a good view through the picture window of apartment 4. We watched Jack adjust the rabbit ears of the TV antenna.

"There!" I exclaimed. The woman who walked over to hand Jack a beer, we knew from photographs, was Sue Lincoln. In a few more moments we saw the two small girls romping on the balcony.

Jack did not stay very long that evening—not long enough to establish adultery evidence. The attorney and I agreed the next day it would be better to keep Jimmy in ignorance until we could gather airtight adultery evidence.

Another week passed, while we kept the couple under close surveillance. One evening as Jack and Sue and the kids drove off for ice cream, Sue made a bad mistake. She sat close to Jack in the car, allowing the children to sit next to the window. While they were driving, she stroked Jack's neck. Signs of affection in public are bad enough legal evidence by themselves—in the presence of children they are much worse.

During the week I called a friend who works for the sheriff's office. Together we went to see the resident manager of the apartment complex, and my friend introduced me as a deputy. We explained that we were investigating the couple in apartment 4 and needed to see a copy of the lease. The resident manager pulled it from the files. It had been signed by Jack and Sue Thornton. They were living together as man and wife. We cautioned the resident manager not to mention our investigation to anyone.

The attorney and I huddled once more. We could probably get Jimmy a divorce on grounds of adultery. But if Jimmy was serious about child custody, the investigation would have to continue, to build up a damning case of continuing adultery, flagrantly flaunted in front of the children. Since Jimmy had already spent a considerable sum on the case, and since we could not guarantee him that he would ultimately win custody, the decision had to be his.

Jimmy came to my office after work. Slowly and carefully, trying to explain the situation in a matter-of-fact manner, I told Jimmy that his wife's lover was his brother-in-law.

Jimmy did not believe me.

We went for a ride to the apartment complex. From the darkness of the parking lot he saw Jack, his wife and his two little girls. Tears rolled down his face. The pitiful man wanted to rush upstairs and embrace his children, and he knew he couldn't.

Slowly, in silence, we drove away.

"Would ... would you do me a big favor?" Jimmy asked.

"What?"

"Would you break it to Amy?"

"All right."

We drove to Jimmy's house. He called Amy and she rushed over. For the second time that evening I explained the details of our investigation. Amy broke down. She and her brother both sobbed uncontrollably.

"What am I going to do?" she wailed. "I want him out. I can't stay with him one more night."

Carefully I explained the situation with regard to Jimmy's children. If he wanted custody we could not yet afford to blow our cover. For the sake of Jimmy's children, Amy agreed to abide by my advice.

"Look," Jimmy said amid his tears. "We've got to tell Mom and Dad."

Amy called Jack, who had returned home and was surprised to find her gone. Her mother was sick, Amy lied. She said she was going to stay with her that night.

A second phone call woke up the parents. The three of us drove to see them, and I explained the situation for a third time. Now confronted by four weeping persons, I was close to some very unprofessional tears myself.

We talked all night long. The Lincolns determined to fight this situation together. By dawn we had evolved a plan.

Jimmy was going to fight doggedly for custody. No one in the family could bear the thought of the little girls growing up amid the tangled domestic affairs of Sue and Jack. My job would be to continue to amass adultery evidence, but Jimmy and his parents also had a job to do. Jimmy would pack up his possessions the next day and move back home. His mother was a retired schoolteacher. She could provide competent daytime care for the two little girls. By the time the case reached court Jimmy could prove that he had established residence in the comfortable environment of his parents' home.

We also had to help Amy get rid of Jack without tipping him to our investigation. We decided that Amy should pick a fight with Jack and make life so intolerable that he would pack up and leave of his own accord. In no case was she to mention the investigation.

My team would perform double duty. Not only would we attempt to win custody of Jimmy's children, but we would also try to win Amy a divorce on grounds of adultery. Her parents agreed to lend Amy the money for Phase II of this incredible case.

When I left the house that morning, exhausted, I had two clients, both in the same family.

"Bastard!" Amy Thornton screamed at her husband.

"Bitch!" Jack yelled back.

The years of unspoken anger and frustration poured out as the couple staged the climactic fight of their ill-fated marriage. Amy had begun the battle by hassling Jack for drinking too much beer, spending too much money and staying out too late. Jack responded with the complaint that Amy was lousy in bed.

Finally Jack said he was leaving.

Amy sensed that he was actually relieved as he packed his bags. The strain of supporting two households must have been terrible. He stormed out of the house and threw his belongings into the trunk of his car.

Linda Goodwin and I were watching from the shadows. Predictably, he led us straight to Sue Lincoln's secret apartment and hauled his suitcases upstairs.

Linda, Guy and I kept the apartment under surveillance almost constantly the next two weeks. We firmly established a pattern of adultery. In the morning Jack would drive Sue and the kids to a babysitter, then drop Sue off at a bus stop. In the evening they would all return to the apartment. They never bothered to hide their affection for each other, even though the children were watching. We had movie film to prove it.

Weeks passed as Jimmy's attorney readied the court papers. He had a long discussion with Jimmy and me concerning the children. In child-custody cases, possession is almost nine-tenths of the law. Jimmy would stand a better chance of gaining permanent custody of his two daughters if he could somehow arrange to already have custody of them at the time of the hearing. Together, the three of us planned a strategy.

From the attorney's office, Jimmy called Sue. It was the first time he had spoken with her in months and he broke down several times during the conversation. Nevertheless, he got his message across: he knew where she and the children were ... he wanted to see the children ... he demanded to take them for the coming weekend ... and he would make things very unpleasant in court if she refused.

Taken completely by surprise, Sue agreed. Neither she nor Jack had as yet hired an attorney.

While Sue scrubbed the children for their visit with

Daddy, others were making careful preparation, too. Jack decided to split, and he found a cabin where he could go fishing for the weekend. Jimmy's attorney obtained several court orders and hired a process server to deliver them first thing Monday morning. Linda, my assistant, took a fistful of money to purchase clothes and toys for the children. I rented a room in a secluded motel.

The little girls went off happily for the weekend with their father, and Jimmy promised his wife that he would return them at 7 P.M. on Sunday. He had absolutely no intention of keeping that promise.

It must have a painful weekend for Sue. She was alone for the first time in months, with nothing to do but think. And when Sunday evening arrived with no sign of Jimmy and the children she began to think the worst.

She must have called her old home number, but that phone was disconnected when Jimmy moved in with his parents. Knowing how close he was to his family, Sue called them. In desperation she even called Amy. They were as puzzled as Sue, for we had deliberately kept the plan secret so that no one in the family would inadvertently tell Sue what was happening.

As panic closed in on Sue, her children were nestled in their beds in a quiet motel room, glad to see their father, not yet missing their mother, and dreaming happily about Linda's selection of new toys.

On Monday morning Sue had an early visitor. The process server handed her papers notifying her that Jimmy was suing for divorce on grounds of adultery and also was asking for custody of the children. The papers named Jack as the co-defendant. The astonished adulteress was also slapped with a restraining order forbidding her to see the children until the case came to court. Later that day Jack was served with papers notifying him that Amy was suing for divorce on grounds of adultery.

And on Monday afternoon Jimmy moved the children to his parents' home.

Child-custody cases are always emotional, but this one seemed to stretch human feelings to the limit. Sue had been dead wrong to leave Jimmy without any explanation, and her cruel act had caused him untold mental anguish. Now it was her turn to suffer. Day after day she drove to her in-laws' home and stood on the front lawn crying and screaming to see her children. Jimmy, on vacation from work, kept the kids inside, hoping that they would not realize what was happening to their mother.

There is something radically wrong with a divorce law that results in this incredible suffering. What's more, the law actually prolonged the agony. The longer the children lived at their grandparents' home, the better the chance of proving the home to be a stable, comfortable environment for them. So Jimmy's attorney used every delaying tactic available to him.

Finally, more than a month after Jimmy had taken the children, this tangled family affair paraded into Domestic Relations Court. The testimony was confusing. Even the judge had difficulty following all the details.

Sue and Jack listened in agony as our evidence unfolded. Painful as it might have been, it would have been far better for the lovers to level with their spouses in the beginning than to go through this public ordeal.

Eventually Sue took the stand in her own defense. In direct examination she attempted to refute our adultery evidence. In her marital trouble she had turned to Jack for emotional support, she admitted, but not sexual support. The loving brother-in-law had helped her find an apartment, and had assisted her in caring for the kids. When Amy kicked him out, he naturally came to her. They had lived together in friendship, but not as lovers.

Jimmy's foxy attorney rose for cross-examination, and in the midst of a series of other unrelated questions, suddenly asked Sue the approximate date of her last intercourse with Jimmy. She answered, truthfully, that it had been about six months. The attorney then asked the court to confirm a rumor that Jack had stupidly mentioned to his estranged wife Amy. According to Jack, Sue had missed her period.

Court was adjourned, pending the results of a pregnancy test. For another week the situation remained tense and unresolved. When the hearing was reconvened, the results of the pregnancy test were read into the record. It was positive: Sue was about two months pregnant. Since the baby could not be Jimmy's, she was a confirmed adulteress.

It cost Sue her two daughters.

The incredible case was still not over. About a month later Linda, Guy and I returned to Domestic Relations Court to testify in the case of *Thornton v. Thornton*. Thankfully, we had the same judge and he was able to follow our testimony more easily the second time around. Child custody was not at issue, and Amy won her divorce rather easily.

Sue and Jack really were in love. They married, and Sue gave birth to Jack's son. Weekends are hectic for this incredible family, for both Sue and Jack have visitation rights with their respective children. The repercussions of this, my most complicated adultery investigation, will be felt for a long time.

13

THE GIRL WITH
THE SEXY UNDERWEAR

Throughout her first fourteen years of marriage Charlotte Farmer wore plain white cotton underpants. She removed them frequently enough, however, for her husband to make her pregnant six times.

The years of washing diapers and screaming kids finally brought a change in Charlotte. She joined a Thursday-night bowling league to get out of the house once a week. She cut her long brown hair into a short, mod style. And she stopped sleeping with her husband.

Steve Farmer was, naturally, upset.

Then one afternoon a rainstorm closed down the construction site where Steve worked, and he came home early. Relaxing with a beer in his hand, he was surprised to find something soft shoved under a sofa cushion. It was a pair of sexy, multicolored bikini underpants.

The husband was both enraged and confused. The sexy underwear confirmed his suspicions that Charlotte had taken a lover. She had even changed the style of her underwear in order to entice the man. But who was he? When did they meet? How could he prove that they were lovers?

Steve realized that he needed advice. He tucked the telltale panties back into their hiding place. The very next day he visited a divorce attorney, who called me in on the case.

Steve, a laborer, could not afford to pay for a lengthy investigation, so we discussed the quickest way to handle the case. He suspected that Charlotte occasionally met her lover at home during the day, but he was sure they were also meeting on Thursday nights after the bowling league. Charlotte had begun to stay out until 2 or 3 A.M. on her bowling nights, claiming that the members of the team always went out for food and beer.

To save Steve some money, we decided to center our investigation on Charlotte's Thursday-night activities.

That week Steve swiped a copy of the weekly schedule for Charlotte's league, which gave us the names of the other four team members—three men and one woman.

Jim Trexler and I sat at the bowling-alley bar watching the players arrive for the early league. As the team assembled we tried to guess which of the men might be Charlotte's lover. Jim thought it must be the slim, quiet fellow who was the team captain. He spoke softly to Charlotte and the other woman on the team as he collected their money for the evening. But I was convinced that the lover had to be another one of the team members, whom I nicknamed Mr. Loudmouth. Big and burly, with a beer belly flopping out over his belt, Mr. Loudmouth was the team clown. He spent the evening paying far more attention to his beer than to his bowling ball. Each time one of the women made a strike he rewarded her with a bear hug.

We killed several hours at the bar waiting for the real games to begin.

As the team was bowling the eighth frame of the final game, we walked outside to my car, which we maneuvered into position about thirty feet away from Charlotte's car. The cold February night made my teeth chatter, so I let the car idle to warm up. The infrared binoculars waited on my lap. We figured that Charlotte would either leave with her lover or meet him somewhere nearby.

We waited about ten minutes before Charlotte came walking toward her car accompanied by a slim shadow. For a moment Jim laughed triumphantly, thinking that the shadow was the team captain, but as the figures passed under a parking lot light we could see that Charlotte was walking with the other woman on the team.

"They're going to meet the guys somewhere else," I assured Jim.

Charlotte started her car and let it idle. Watching through the binoculars I saw the other girl slide over toward the center of the seat. Charlotte threw her arms around the woman and kissed her passionately.

"Oh my God!" I said, focusing in on the action. Jim could not see what was happening.

"What's going on?" he said.

"Jim, you wouldn't believe it. I'm going to try to get a little closer."

I eased the engine into gear and slipped my foot off the brake pedal to let the car creep closer as I continued to peer through the binoculars.

Bang! The car jarred to a stop and lifted us right off the seats. I had run right into a light pole! The two women broke from their embrace and looked around. Red-faced, I backed the car away out of sight.

Five minutes later Charlotte drove off, and I tried to follow discreetly. They parked outside an apartment building and once again embraced passionately. This time Jim saw the action through the binoculars too, while the women made out together for about fifteen minutes.

After leaving the other woman, Charlotte drove herself to a house in Cheverly, Maryland. A couple of cars were sitting in the driveway when she entered. We tried to sneak close to a window, but we were driven off by the yelping of a couple of small dogs.

There was nothing we could do but wait outside and

imagine what was happening inside. Around 2 A.M. Charlotte came out of the house and drove home alone.

The next afternoon Steve came to my office after work. When I told him what we had observed he broke down in tears. He just could not believe that his wife was a lesbian.

"I've already talked to your lawyer about this," I told him. "Steve, I'm afraid that homosexuality is not adultery. We can try to get you a divorce on grounds of mental cruelty, but unless we catch her with another man we can't prove adultery. And from what I saw last night I don't think we're going to catch her with another man."

We had to get better evidence of homosexuality for Steve to get out of his disagreeable marriage. He had taken out a loan to pay for this investigation, and he had just about enough money left for one more night of surveillance. He begged me to try to gather sufficient evidence on Charlotte's next bowling night.

The following Thursday Jim and I once again watched the bowling team play its match. This time we ignored the men and paid a lot more attention to the other woman in Charlotte's life. She was slightly built, with medium-length brown hair. Her face was attractive in a little-girl sort of way. Tight tan slacks covered her slim bottom. Now that we were looking closely, there seemed to be a definite spark flying between the two women.

Later we again saw the two of them make out in the parking lot. We followed them back to the girl's apartment, and this time Charlotte went inside with her.

I quickly taped the door.

The apartment was on the ground floor, next to the front entrance. If I stepped over the iron railing and leaned out over the end of the porch I could peer around the edge of the Venetian blinds. Naturally it was impossible to hold this position for very long, but Jim and I managed to sneak a look inside each time we checked the tape. The girls were sitting together on the sofa watching television.

There is something about the sight of two women making love to one another that fascinates me. I *had* to get a better look at the inside of that apartment!

Down a hill from the apartment building I could see the lights of a delicatessen. About 11:30 its lights went out, and I left Jim to watch the apartment while I trotted down to the store. In the back I found what I was looking for—two empty orange crates. I lugged them back up the hill.

We spotted a good vantage point on the side of the building behind some bushes where we could look through another opening in the blinds. We had an excellent view of the sofa.

The two women were still watching television. Their slacks were in a heap on the floor. They were dressed only in blouses and underpants. Charlotte was wearing her customary plain white cotton pants. Her girlfriend was wearing multicolored bikini pants similar to the ones Steve said he had found in the sofa. They were drinking beer.

All four of us ignored the television program when Charlotte slid her hand inside her lover's underpants and began playing with her. Then she unbuttoned the girl's blouse, revealing small bra-less breasts. Charlotte leaned over and nibbled on them.

Charlotte's lover got up from the sofa and turned off the television. We watched her walk across the room clad only in her colorful panties to place a stack of records on the stereo. Then she returned to the sofa, unbuttoned Charlotte's blouse and removed her bra. She eased Charlotte down on the sofa and pulled off the plain white panties. As we watched from our orange crates, the two women made love. It was 3:30 in the morning before Charlotte left the house.

Early the next week our report was ready, and Steve's attorney filed the divorce papers. On the day that Charlotte was served with the subpoena she packed up her bags and moved into her girlfriend's apartment. She left her six children behind.

Charlotte did not even bother to hire an attorney, for there was nothing that she cared to salvage from her marriage. It was as though she had just become a different person. To this day Steve is dumbfounded by the sudden transformation.

I spoke to him some time after the divorce, and he told me that Charlotte had moved to California with her girlfriend. They were living in a women's commune.

Steve is still looking for a new mother for his six children.

14

SOLO JOB

Day after dreary day Dr. Amos Norris left his home in southern Maryland at 7 A.M. in order to arrive in time for his 8 A.M. shift at Walter Reed Army Medical Center. But, after twenty years of unswerving devotion to his schedule, he inexplicably began to leave the house at 4:30 in the morning. Coupled with fact that he no longer slept in the same bed with his wife, Emma, the situation seemed highly suspicious. Emma decided to hire a detective.

A friend of a friend referred her to me.

Emma is about fifty, a pudgy, rather unattractive woman. Amos had always been the core of her life. Emma, now distraught, had no one to confide in.

As part of the first interview with a new client I aways suggest that the investigation remain a total secret. The client invariably feels upset and isolated, and the temptation is great to discuss the case with a close friend.

This time my warning proved to be a wise one.

Amos is tall and slim. He has arrived at that age where he can attract respect and attention. His double position of authority—as a doctor and Army officer—seemed to hold a special appeal. The surface facts all pointed to the existence of a girlfriend.

Normally a new case puts me into a good mood. Business is business, and every cash-paying customer brightens my day. But I did not look forward to beginning surveillance at 4 A.M.

Rubbing sand from our eyes, Guy Morgan and I sat in two cars outside Amos's home the next morning. The focus of our attention was a little Volkswagen that Amos cared for like a son. Emma was not allowed to drive it; she did not even have a key for it.

Exactly at 4:30 the doctor left his home. Guy and I cautiously followed him out to the main highway, where he plodded along at a respectable fifty-five miles per hour. Suddenly he pulled off on the shoulder of the road, and I drove on past him. By radio I instructed Guy to pick up the surveillance as soon as Amos started up once again.

But Amos didn't move. Guy watched from the parking lot of a diner down the road. He saw Amos open the trunk of his car, which is up front in a VW, and take something out of it. Now he was just sitting in the car.

A half hour passed, and Amos remained parked by the side of the road. Fighting my sleepiness, I waited for something to happen. Finally Amos started his car and drove another couple of miles. Guy reported that he pulled off on the side of the road once more, and I doubled back to pick up surveillance.

Nothing happened. Amos merely sat there behind the wheel for another half hour. The long straight road made it impossible for us to get close enough to observe his actions. I drove past a couple of times but he appeared to be merely reading.

Amos stopped four times by the side of the road that morning and finally arrived at Walter Reed precisely at eight. Our surveillance produced a big zero.

I wondered if he was merely using the quiet early-morning hours to catch up on his professional reading.

For the next two weeks Amos led us on a chase that was exasperating, expensive and extremely dull. Each day his routine was identical. He would stop three or four times on his way to work, grab what appeared to be books and magazines from the trunk of the car, and sit behind the wheel reading them. There was not the slightest hint of adultery.

But Emma could sense that something was very wrong in their relationship. She continued to pay for the investigation with huge chunks of cash drawn secretly from the couple's life savings. We needed more than money, however. We really needed to know what was in the trunk of Amos's Volkswagen. I considered attempting to pick the lock, but Amos always kept the car parked in a busy lot at Walter Reed, or locked in his attached garage at home.

Finally, in the third week of our surveillance, Amos began to make mistakes. Up until now he seemed to choose his morning parking spots at random. He finally developed a pattern. He picked out one spot in particular and parked there every morning. It was well off the highway, nestled next to a wooded bank. One morning I was waiting in the woods when he arrived.

In the dim light of the rising sun I trained my binoculars on him. He removed his books and magazines from the trunk. I was still a bit too far away to see them clearly as he sat behind the wheel reading. I was not too far away, however, to see him begin masturbating.

We had at least determined that Amos was not studying technical papers that early in the morning!

His next mistake came that very night when he announced to Emma that he was going to take a long hot bath. As he eased into the suds Emma grabbed his car keys and made a mad dash to a nearby store, where she had the trunk key copied. She managed to arrive back home before Amos had finished soaking.

She was forced to wait impatiently for nearly a week before Amos borrowed her car to drive some other doctors to a meeting. He left the Volkswagen at home. Emma, unknown to me, opened the trunk of the car.

I was at home when my office called—a hysterical woman demanded to talk to me. That in itself is not unusual, but when I heard it was Emma I was especially interested.

I met the sobbing woman at her home, and without any explanation she handed me a notebook binder. Inside were a series of nude photographs of a very attractive middle-aged woman. She must have been about forty-five years of age, and about thirty-eight inches in the bust. The thick book contained photographs of the woman in every naked position imaginable—from the artistic to the raunchy.

My client was screaming and crying, I thought, beyond the point of rationality. Certainly it was a shock to find the sexy photos, but she *had* expected that something was going on.

"It's Andrea," she screamed. "My best friend! We go to the commissary together all the time!"

Through Emma's tears, the story unfolded. Andrea's husband had been an infantry officer, killed in combat in Vietnam. Prior to that the four had often met socially, and they had continued their friendship after the death of Andrea's husband. I was very thankful I had persuaded Emma not to confide in her friends.

"How do you think he got the photos?" I asked.

"He's ... he's got a darkroom in the basement," Emma sobbed. "He's always puttering around down there. I never bother to watch what he's doing."

I forced Emma to look once more at the photographs. "How recent do you think these are?"

Emma studied the inviting face attached to the naked body. "A couple of months," she said. "No more. Andrea got her hair cut about then, the way it is here."

Emma's shock turned quickly to anger. She vowed to confront Amos with the evidence that very night.

I eventually was able to talk her out of it. As suspicious as the photos were, they were still not proof of adultery. Amos did not appear in any of the photos. He could claim that he merely took them for artistic value. He could even claim he found them!

Finally Emma agreed that she would rather have the long-term satisfaction of a divorce than the short-term satisfaction of watching Amos squirm that night. Together we placed the photos back into the Volkswagen, next to several pornographic novels also stashed there.

Our immediate problem was to figure out when and where Amos was meeting Andrea. I was also quite concerned that Emma's shock might show through—if not to Amos, then to Andrea. So I persuaded Emma to leave town for the weekend. She flew to visit her parents in Missouri.

Guy and I staked out the Volkswagen at its Walter Reed parking spot about noon on Friday. Amos evidently had plans for the weekend, for he left work about 1:30 and drove leisurely up the Baltimore-Washington Parkway to the large Army base at Fort Meade, Maryland. He parked and entered the PX. I followed curiously and watched him buy a large quantity of film and flash cubes.

Emma had kept her cool, but I suspect that her nervousness had shown through, because Amos then pulled one of the oldest tricks in the book. Coming out of the PX he removed a slip of paper from his pocket. He walked to a phone booth and dialed a number while looking carefully at the paper. There apparently was no answer, so he replaced the phone, crumpled the bit of paper and tossed it casually into a trash basket.

He watched the trash bin from his car for twenty minutes, figuring that no private detective could resist that crumpled phone number. Guy and I watched him watch the trash bin. Now that we had seen him buy the film we figured his model would show up soon.

A few minutes after 3 P.M. a gray Opel pulled into the parking lot and stopped near Amos's Volkswagen. An attractive woman got out, and I recognized her even with her clothes on. She pulled an overnight bag out of the car and stepped into the Volkswagen. Photographer and model drove off together.

Confident that he was not being followed, Amos drove easily up the parkway while Andrea rubbed his neck. The lovers headed directly to a motel near Baltimore. When Amos walked up to the registration desk I was already there and witnessed him registering as a fictitious Mr. and Mrs. He picked up a key for room 117.

Andrea was waiting outside. Though she obviously enjoyed posing for pictures, she was unaware that Guy was snapping a beautiful sequence that showed Amos walking to her from the motel lobby, helping her out of the car, and ushering her into room 117.

We taped the door and established our normal routine of motel surveillance. From time to time throughout the evening we could see the flashes of Amos's camera explode past the edge of the curtains.

In the morning the happy couple left the motel hand in hand and drove back to Fort Meade, pursued by another happy couple of investigators. Andrea got into her car and followed Amos south onto the Baltimore-Washington Parkway. Our caravan wound lazily toward Washington and into the parking lot of a hotel only a block away from the U.S. Capitol Building.

Guy and I were able to register in a room just across the the hall from them. The door, conveniently, was fitted with a peephole that provided us with an easy means of surveillance.

That evening the couple walked out hand in hand and strolled around the reflecting pool near the Capitol. Then they shared dinner at a dark, intimate restaurant, where they kissed a few times.

After they returned to the hotel room, flashes of light under the door indicated that Amos was photographing more beautiful scenery.

Emma's attorney appreciates good photography almost as much as Amos. We already had an array of stills that—while not as stimulating as Amos's homemade pornography—would cause considerable trouble in court. Since we were close to my Washington office, however, I decided to pick up my movie camera and try for some action shots.

Sunday morning, after spending the night with Amos in a room guarded by a matchstick, Andrea left alone. I suspected this precaution, since they had driven both cars. But thanks to a bit of luck and an icepick, the left rear tire of Andrea's car was flat. She had no choice but to return to the hotel room and ask Amos for help.

A full reel of 16mm movie film shows them emerging from the hotel doorway together, fixing the flat, and kissing goodbye. The camera even caught Amos administering a therapeutic pat to the left rear of Andrea—which, I might add, was not flat at all.

Emma flew back on Monday and I met her at the airport. We immediately drove to Walter Reed, where she removed the nude photos of Andrea and the printed pornography from the trunk of her husband's car. Amos discovered the theft quickly and left home that very night.

Emma could no longer control herself. She called her "best friend" and poured out her anger. The sobbing Andrea said she never meant to hurt Emma, but she and Amos were very much in love. Poor Emma hung up and faced the prospect of long, lonely nights.

We had such a pile of evidence that Amos would have been foolish to go to court: the case would have been far too embarrassing to his career. And, of course, poor Andrea faced the prospect of sitting in the courtroom while her porno poses were introduced as evidence.

The uncontested divorce cost Amos his home and most of his furnishings. He received custody of his clothes. a sofa bed. his Volkswagen and his darkroom equipment.

15

THE KIDNAP CAPER

It is not my job to make moral judgments about my clients and my subjects. In almost all cases of marital breakdown, both husband and wife bear a share of the guilt. Anyone connected with divorce cases will assure you, however, that often the ones who suffer the most are completely innocent. Divorce is a nightmare for children.

The case of Hank and Ellen Henderson does not involve adultery, but it was one of the most bitter divorces I have ever witnessed. And it put the two young daughters through an experience they will probably remember with horror for the rest of their lives.

An attorney called me one day with a case. It was Evelyn Spencer, the hard-nosed divorce attorney, who is an expert on the law but is somewhat callous about her client's feelings. Evelyn runs a case with an iron hand, and I had no choice but to follow her instructions to the letter.

The details have a familiar ring. Hank Henderson is a high-ranking civilian official who works closely with the Navy Department. His job often requires him to spend a month or two overseas on temporary duty. He returned one afternoon from a particularly long trip to find that his apartment in Norfolk, Virginia, was virtually empty. Only a bed and a few kitchen utensils were there.

His wife, Ellen, also was gone, along with their two daughters.

Hank called the police. A brief investigation revealed that Ellen had cleaned out the joint savings account six weeks earlier. That action clearly labeled this a domestic, not a criminal case, so the police dropped it. Hank was forced to deal with the situation privately.

He contacted Evelyn, who immediately called me.

Hank could not conceive of his wife's committing adultery, but he did acknowledge that over the past year they had been getting more and more remote. Both had suspected the marriage was headed for divorce.

But Hank was understandably bitter that Ellen had left so mysteriously. He missed his children. Evelyn warned that it would be difficult to get custody of them, but Hank wanted to try.

Our first job, of course, was to find them. Jim Metz and I flew to Minneapolis, where we staked out the homes of Ellen's parents and other relatives. There was no sign of our subjects. We returned to the Norfolk area and kept Ellen's friends under a similar close watch.

After three weeks we had found nothing.

In desperation we checked out various vacation spots that the Hendersons had visited over the years. Hank told us that they had once spent two weeks at a motel in Nag's Head, North Carolina, and we drove there to see if Ellen might have returned.

In the motel parking lot we spotted Ellen's blue Mustang. A couple of hours later Ellen and the children emerged from the motel and drove off in the car.

I called the attorney, and Evelyn decided not to tell Hank anything until we had watched his wife long enough to determine if she had a lover. For the next three days Jim and I kept her under a very strict surveillance. She had been on her own with the children for over two months and was confident that she had escaped detection. She was easy to follow; there was no evidence of a boyfriend. This appeared to be a simple case of desertion.

Evelyn wanted Hank to have custody of the children

when the case went to court, but that meant he would have to snatch them away from their mother.

Several things happened simultaneously. Evelyn broke the news to the grieving father. Jim continued to keep an eye on our subject while I called my Washington office. I sent two assistants to Wilmington, Delaware, where they registered into a motel under the names of William Pearce and James Metz. Another assistant, Linda Goodwin, drove down to Norfolk, picked up Hank, and brought him to meet us in Nag's Head. They arrived on a Thursday morning.

The attorney had explained the situation to Hank. He knew he had to get his children, but he was nervous about it. As soon as he saw me the distraught man asked if I would grab the kids for him. No way! A father cannot be accused of kidnaping his own children, but a private detective can get a life sentence for such an act. He would have to do the job himself—though we would help him any way we could.

Throughout the afternoon and late into the night we planned the job, and by Friday morning we were ready. Linda drove off alone to a spot about a half mile north of town. She parked on a side street near an apartment building that had an underground parking lot, facing her car toward the street, where she could alert us if a police patrol car was headed in our direction. She also began to monitor the frequency of the local police radio.

At 8:30 Friday morning Ellen left the hotel with her children and drove a few blocks to a restaurant. The three of them went inside. I checked on them long enough to see that they were ordering breakfast.

We had to work fast. I told Hank to disconnect the distributor cap from his wife's car. Nervous and stuttering, Hank claimed he didn't know how. He wanted me to do it.

Cussing under my breath, I showed him the distributor cap on my own car and pushed him toward the parking lot, where he managed to disable Ellen's transportation.

Then we waited—kids can eat very slowly. Twenty minutes passed. Our hearts were pounding. Hank was pale. When he saw Ellen go to the cash register near the door I eased my car up close to the entrance, parking it at an angle toward the street. Jim and I got out of the car and stood near the entrance.

Ellen opened the door for her children to leave the restaurant and turned to latch it shut behind her.

"Daddy! Daddeee!"

The little girls squealed with delight as their father hopped out of the back seat. They ran to hug him and he lifted them off the ground, one under each arm. Like a fullback sniffing the end zone, he ran for the back seat of my car.

I can recall the next few seconds as a slow-motion sequence—a sort of instant replay. Ellen was stunned for a moment. Her face registered horror and disbelief. Then her mouth opened in an earsplitting scream, and she ran toward her children.

Jim and I both stepped between her and the car, but she ran us down like an enraged linebacker and grabbed at Hank. Her hand caught a piece of his shirt, and ripped it off his back. Long red streaks appeared where her nails cut into his flesh. Jim and I grabbed for her arms while she kicked viciously at her husband's shins. She was cursing. Hank was crying. The children were screaming in terror.

Suddenly a car pulled up next to us and a confused couple tried to assess the situation. Without abandoning her attack on Hank, Ellen screamed to the bystanders, "Please help me! Call the police! They're kidnaping my children!"

The driver jumped out of his car. He assumed a boxing crouch, but he didn't know whether to attack Hank, Jim or me. I ran toward him and flashed my ID.

"Look, we're detectives," I sputtered. "Everything's okay. Just mind your own business and stay back."

Thank God, he was no hero. My warning scared him

off. None of the other horrified onlookers who had gathered in the parking lot attempted to help.

Jim pushed Ellen to the side and Hank managed to scramble into the back seat with the kids. I can still see the car door slamming shut at the very instant the mother reached out in desperation for her children. By perhaps half an inch Ellen's fingers escaped being crushed in the door. Hank locked it before she could pull on the door handle.

I was the last to jump into the car. Ellen grabbed my arm as I was trying to get inside. Viciously she dug her nails into me. Then she tore at my hair and kicked my legs. I had no choice but to push her aside. She fell to the ground screaming. I jumped into the car and left two long lines of black rubber marks on the street.

Hank was sobbing. The kids were yelling. They looked out the back window to see their mother running after the car shouting hysterically.

Suddenly Ellen remembered her own car and ran to it. If Hank had not stolen the distributor cap Ellen surely would have killed someone in her haste to follow us.

A half mile down the road we ducked into a back street and met Linda. Hank, the girls and I all hopped into Linda's car. Jim ditched my car in the apartment parking lot and lost himself on the beach for a few days.

Linda told us that the police radio already had a description of my car, including the license number. Calmly, Linda eased her car onto the main highway and drove in the one direction the police would not suspect— back toward the restaurant!

Hank kept himself and the children down low. I ducked down, too, but now I understand why a criminal returns to the scene of his crime. I could not resist a peek as we passed the restaurant. The place was overflowing with police cars. Hundreds of spectators milled around the parking lot. Linda had to slow the car to a crawl in order to ease past.

She drove carefully, never exceeding the speed limit.

When we were about fifty miles outside of town, we stopped and bought the kids about $100 worth of toys. That cheered them up considerably. We got Hank a new shirt to replace the one his wife had ripped off his back.

Friday night we registered Hank and the kids at a motel outside of Atlanta, Georgia. Linda and I drove all night to return to Norfolk.

On Saturday Jim called from Nag's Head. There was an all-points bulletin out for us, but the descriptions of our appearance were poor. There was no mention in the newspapers that the case was domestic, so we were sure Ellen had not yet told the police the kidnaper was her husband.

I called Hank, who was scheduled to fly home with the kids on Sunday. I asked him, before he left for the airport, to call the Nag's Head police and explain the domestic nature of the kidnaping. He was to give them his attorney's name for verification. He did so, and the police agreed to drop the kidnaping charges. But they had traced the license plate number to me, and they demanded that I return to face assault charges filed by Ellen.

I shoved that minor problem to the back of my mind and concentrated on the business at hand. Linda and I met Hank and his children at the airport and escorted them safely to a local motel.

Owing to the furor we had created, Evelyn had decided to rush the case through court. She was going to file divorce papers on Monday morning, but she first needed a list of all the items that Ellen had left behind when she moved out. Linda and I drove over to the Hendersons' apartment to compile the list.

Meanwhile the desperate mother was determined to find her children. The first place she decided to look, logically, was her former apartment. She arrived while Linda and I were inside. Fortunately Hank had changed the lock. Ellen rattled her key back and forth unsuccessfully while I sneaked a look through the peephole. I was horrified at the thought of confronting that wild lady once more!

Ellen realized that her key was useless and was about to leave when a nosy neighbor came into the hallway and said that two people had just gone inside. As we listened through the door Ellen said she would watch the entrance while the neighbor called the police.

Linda and I scrambled out a back window and drove away as police sirens screamed toward the apartment.

Ellen was served with papers on Monday. On Wednesday everyone shuffled into court for a preliminary hearing to determine temporary custody of the children. The whole terrible scene in Nag's Head was replayed for the judge.

His honor glared at Evelyn. He knew her aggressive style was responsible for the kidnaping. He reprimanded Hank for the incident but admitted that he understood the motives.

Hank stood no chance of gaining permanent custody. There was not a shred of adultery evidence. And the pressures of his job took him away from home too often. So the judge awarded custody to the mother, but he issued strict orders for her to remain in Virginia. He allowed Hank to take the children every weekend that he wanted to and to visit with them any evening he desired.

Only one detail remained, and that was the sticky question of the assault charge in Nag's Head. I needed a vacation anyway, so on a Friday I drove my family to the resort. While they hit the beach I stopped in to see the district attorney. I knew I did not even vaguely resemble the eyewitness descriptions. What's more, I had an affidavit signed by Jim Metz, stating that he had been with me on an investigation in Wilmington, Delaware, on the day of the kidnaping. I had a photocopy of the motel registration card to prove it.

The district attorney knew that his case was weak. He examined the documents I offered and sat back in his chair.

"Okay," he said finally. "I'm satisfied that you didn't do it."

I thanked him and turned to leave.

"Pearce!" he said.

"Yes."

"Don't do it again!"

16

OUT WITH THE BOYS

He had been watching me all afternoon, waiting to catch me alone. When Jim Metz went to the bathroom he saw his chance. Casually he took a sip of his imported beer, rose from the table at the back of the room, and walked in my direction.

"Hi," he said cheerfully. "Would you care to dance?"

What could I do? In the three hours we had been sitting at the bar not one man had refused an offer to dance. To turn down the invitation would arouse suspicion.

"Sure."

Just my luck . . . it was a slow number. The fellow held me close. It took all my professional self-control to refrain from busting him in the mouth. My mind raced much faster than the music. What if one of my friends from the vice squad happened to drop in? They often checked the scene in Washington's gay bars. The word would spread around the courthouse that I had become a homosexual.

Then I remembered Jim. I saw him come out of the bathroom and return to the bar. He looked confused when he saw my seat empty. His eyes searched throughout the club until he saw me on the dance floor. A big grin covered his face, and I saw him race back to the bathroom to hide his laughter.

Finally the music ended, and a fast number began.

"Want to dance this one, too?" my companion asked.

"Gee, I better not," I said. "My friend might get mad."

"Yeah. I understand. See you around."

My dance partner returned to a table in the back of the room, where five men sat drinking beer. One of them was the subject of our investigation.

I watched our subject, Pete Barnard, as he chatted with the "man" of the hour. George Gregory's photo was plastered all over the walls of this famous Washington gay bar, known as The Lost and Found. George had just won the monthly contest as the most beautiful transvestite in town. Our subject seemed to be on very good terms with the lovely young beauty queen.

As I watched Pete light George's cigarette, someone whispered in my ear. "Wanna dance?"

Oh, no, not again! I thought. I turned to see Jim's face leering down at me.

"Go to hell," I said. "Just because you're not pretty enough to be asked, don't get jealous."

We settled back, continuing to keep our attention upon Pete and his friend, gorgeous George. They danced and drank together for about five hours that Sunday afternoon.

Eventually the beer drove me to the john while Jim continued the surveillance. To prevent the walls from becoming soiled with graffiti, the management had installed a blackboard over the urinals so messages could be chalked onto it. In a moment of inspiration I scrawled, "Jim Metz, meet me at the bar at 6:30. Tonight's plans have changed. Your love, Don."

When Jim saw the note later he cussed me out for leaving his name in the public john. We were even.

By early evening we had followed our subject and his friends to another gay bar known as The Pier Nine, located on the Washington, D.C., waterfront. There they ate dinner, drank and danced some more. I made a point of remaining out of sight behind the bar, which is located on an upper level away from the tables, so my dancing partner would not spot me a second time.

But my biggest problem was not how to avoid dancing with the guy; it was how to tell Pete's wife what we had discovered about her husband during the long day of surveillance.

Elizabeth Barnard was a naïve little rich girl. She had married Pete two years earlier, just after her graduation from a New England finishing school. Pete had willingly accepted his new father-in-law's offer to set him up in business, and his posh canine beauty salon was one of the new "in" spots for the rich poodle owners who lived in Washington's Georgetown neighborhood.

Elizabeth's parents also gave the couple a new home near Mt. Vernon, valued at more than $100,000.

Soon after he had built the pet salon into a profitable business, Pete stopped sleeping with Elizabeth. He spent a lot of time away from home, most often on Thursday evenings and on weekends. Elizabeth was certain that he had a girlfriend.

Her parents recommended the city's top divorce lawyer, who, in turn, hired me to investigate.

During my initial interview with Elizabeth I became quickly convinced that Pete did not have a girlfriend. The photo of her husband showed a very handsome but effeminate face. Pete's hair was long and carefully styled. With lipstick and eye makeup on, he would have appeared to be a woman.

As usual I asked Elizabeth if her husband had mentioned any particular clubs and restaruants that we could keep under surveillance. She listed several places that he talked about, among them The Lost and Found and The Pier Nine. All of them were gay bars—and proud of it. However, I was careful not to mention this to Elizabeth.

After the first surveillance confirmed my suspicions, the attorney and I had a long discussion. We could not, of course, win a divorce for Elizabeth on grounds of adultery.

In order to prove cruelty we would have to establish a long and continuous pattern of homosexual activity. A judge is reluctant to label someone a homosexual unless the evidence is overwhelming. Even though Elizabeth was impatiently awaiting the results of our investigation, we decided not to tell her until we had further proof.

So on the following Thursday evening Jim and I tailed Pete from his salon to a fashionable high-rise apartment building in Bethesda, Maryland. He opened the main entrance with a key and walked inside. We watched him step into the elevator. Locked outside without a key, we had to hang around until another tenant emerged from the entrance. I grabbed the door before it could slam shut.

Our subject was somewhere in one of the building's 450 apartments, and our only clue was the name of the transvestite he had been dancing with at The Lost and Found. Unfortunately the 450 mailboxes in the lobby only listed the last names of the tenants, and there were five Gregorys! We copied down the apartment numbers and taped all five doors.

Then we watched the building until 2:30 in the morning, when Pete finally walked out and drove off in his Porsche. We had to wait another twenty impatient minutes until we could get back inside the building. We checked all five doors, and on only one of them, an apartment on the twelfth floor, was the tape dislodged.

Late the following Sunday afternoon we watched from our cars as Pete left his home. As soon as he headed up the Capitol Beltway toward Bethesda I raced on ahead. I was waiting behind an exit door on the twelfth floor when he walked to the Gregory apartment. He knocked, and I saw the transvestite kiss him at the door. All that evening Jim and I hovered in the hallway, concealing our surveillance behind the exit door but frequently daring to sneak down to the apartment and listen. We heard pots and pans rattle, and we could smell gourmet cooking. I was checking the tape on the door about 7:30 when I heard the security chain rattle. I ran quickly for cover and told Jim they were leaving. Jim rushed down the stairwell in an attempt to beat the elevator down the twelve floors. I decided to help him. Casually I walked down the hallway behind the gay couple and waited with them for the elevator. As the car lurched into motion I pretended to lose my balance. Reaching out to brace myself, I "accidentally" pushed the buttons to stop the elevator at several other floors.

"Oops," I said, as Pete and his lover rolled their eyes. "Sorry."

The ploy gave Jim time enough to grab a camera and position himself to take photos of the couple walking out of the building hand in hand.

We followed them on a winding drive through Washington to a small apartment complex in Alexandria, Virginia. Jim taped the door of the second-story apartment they entered, while I watched the activity that was taking place on the balcony. Several young men were sitting outside drinking beer. All were handsome and well-dressed. I recognized one of them as the young man I had danced with.

When Jim joined me in my car I explained to him that I knew these particular apartments very well. Only three months earlier I had conducted an investigation there. A newspaper boy had been accused of peeping into the window of a ground-floor apartment very near to the one we were watching. The father was sure his son was innocent and hired me to discover the identity of the real Peeping Tom. I had suspected the janitor, and sure enough, I caught him peering through a window at 3 A.M. I managed to snap several infrared photos that persuaded the old man to plead guilty, clearing the newspaper boy of suspicion.

As darkness fell and the men moved inside I was interested in getting a better look at the festivities. I remembered that the janitor's storage room contained a ladder that would reach to the second-story windows. Jim and I sneaked over, picked the lock and brought the ladder back. Cautiously I climbed up to the second story and peered around the edge of the large picture window into the living room.

It was packed with young men. Many were holding drinks and a few were dancing slowly in the middle of the floor. Over in a corner one man was sitting on the lap of another, kissing him with abandon. Pete was chatting with my former dancing partner. I eased back down the ladder and sent Jim up for a look.

In a few minutes my assistant came back down. "Pete just went into a bedroom with another guy," he whispered.

We moved the ladder around the corner of the building and positioned it near the bedroom window. After waiting fifteen minutes to give the couple a chance to get started, I sneaked up the ladder.

Both men were completely naked, lying on the bed with the door to the room unashamedly open. Enough light filtered in from the living room so that I could easily watch as they made love.

Quickly but quietly I scrambled down the ladder. I wanted Jim's corroborating testimony before the two men finished their sex act.

But as my foot hit the ground I felt a strong hand clamp down upon my shoulder.

"Hold it right there, fella!" a harsh voice commanded.

I looked up to see an angry man in a blue uniform staring at me in disgust. Jim was pinned to the wall by another uniform.

"What's going on?" the policeman demanded.

It took several minutes to explain the gun that the officer found in my belt, and several more minutes to explain the ladder. One of the neighbors, it seems, had called the police to report the return of the Peeping Tom.

As I told the officer my story I could see him glance up to the apartment. I knew he wanted to climb up and see for himself, but he resisted the temptation. He said he would not arrest us, but he would have to file a full report. If the apartment management wanted to press charges, we could be in trouble.

As the policemen left they ordered us to return the ladder and behave ourselves for the rest of the evening.

We took the ladder back but we certainly had no intention of behaving ourselves. As soon as the police car left Jim and I discussed how we might get the names of the men who leased the apartment. They could then be subpoenaed as co-subjects.

"If only I could get inside the apartment," I muttered.

By midnight most of the guests had left, but Pete was still inside. With my ever-present icepick I flattened a tire on Pete's beautiful Porsche. When he and George Gregory came out to the car about 1 A.M. they were upset to see the flat. They ran back to the apartment and brought the others down to change the tire by committee.

And, as I had hoped, they left the apartment door unlocked. Working quickly, I searched the apartment for the names of the tenants. On a kitchen counter I found a stack of mail and copied the names of three men who had received letters at that address. When I sneaked back outside the five men were still working on the tire.

On Tuesday I met Elizabeth for lunch at the Mayflower Hotel. When I made the date I promised her a full report of our work. I poured a couple of drinks into her and then told her the details of our first surveillance. I explained that we had followed Pete to The Lost and Found, where he had joined several other men at a table.

Elizabeth was relieved. "He didn't go there with a girl?" she asked.

"Elizabeth, here's the story. The Lost and Found is a very well-known place for gay people to meet other gay people."

"You don't mean to tell me he's gay!?"

"Let me just tell you what we observed." Elizabeth listened without a visible trace of emotion. But when I finished she started crying softly. She excused herself for several minutes. When she returned she was cool and composed. Her finishing-school polish was once again glistening brightly.

"I guess I should have known," she said. "He was always going over to see George. I thought it was an excuse to meet a girl." She bit her lip. "If only it was another girl, at least I could try to compete."

After lunch we went to see her attorney. He prepared the papers and had them served.

Pete moved out to take up permanent residence in George's apartment. Since there was a considerable amount of jointly owned property to be divided, Pete did not want the settlement to be influenced by an admission of homosexuality. He and his attorney planned to attack the validity of our reports when the case went to court.

The most damning evidence was what I had observed while gaping into the second-story apartment. During a pretrial deposition the attorney conducted a vigorous cross-examination, trying to catch me in a lie.

But I was telling the truth.

Elizabeth's cagy attorney had an ace in the hole. After the defense attorney had spent several hours trying unsuccessfully to tear down my story, Elizabeth's lawyer showed him a copy of the county police report of the investigation of the Peeping Tom complaint.

When Pete's attorney realized that the county police were ready to corroborate my testimony, he advised his client to settle out of court. Quickly.

Pete was allowed to keep his business, which he had carefully registered completely in his own name. But Elizabeth retained full ownership of the $100,000 home and most of the other assets.

She is still a rich girl, but she is no longer naïve.

17

TRIPLE PLAY

She had a paper bag in her hand. "I brought you a present," she said as she pulled a bottle of wine and two glasses from the bag. "If you're not busy, I'd like to have a drink with you. I need to talk."

I opened the bottle and poured out two generous portions.

Carolyn DeForest had hired me two days earlier to investigate her husband. We talked for three hours that first day, and I knew she was holding back some vital piece of information. She had protested too vigorously that she had no idea why her husband's behavior had changed so quickly.

Chick DeForest is a very important man in the local government of one of Washington's suburban communities. He had married Carolyn fifteen years earlier and had been a loving husband for fourteen years. Suddenly he had begun to stay out late at night, never explaining why. When Carolyn questioned him about his activities she was rewarded with a slap across the face. They had not made love for three months.

That fact alone was difficult to believe. Carolyn is a very beautiful woman who appears much younger than her thirty-six years. For nearly a decade she has worked as the executive secretary to the pastor of one of the largest Protestant churches in the Washington area. Her breasts, however, are extremely irreligious. She tries to keep them hidden inside demure necklines, but it is a losing battle. Chick had to have a very special reason for ignoring his wife, and I sensed that Carolyn knew what it was.

"Cheers," I said to Carolyn's breasts, raising my glass.

She smiled and gulped her wine. Finally, when the bottle was half empty, she leveled with me.

Carolyn and Chick had become close friends with another couple, Ginnie and Warren Long. Ginnie is a schoolteacher; Warren a traveling salesman. The four enjoyed each other's company, and the previous summer they had all vacationed together at Ocean City, Maryland, staying in the condominium apartment of a friend.

One night the four of them were sitting around in the apartment drinking wine. As the bacchanal progressed Warren began to kiss his wife passionately, and Chick began to make out with Carolyn. The petting became heavy, and eventually the couples stripped and began to make love. The Longs were entwined on the sofa while the DeForests were busy on the shag rug.

Warren looked over and suggested to Chick that they switch partners. Suddenly Warren was on top of and inside of Carolyn. She enjoyed it immensely, she confessed to me with a guilty look. She had always been attracted to Warren.

But the next day life seemed unbearable. Guilt haunted her every thought. No one dared mention the experience as they basked in the sun of the beach. Then nighttime came, and the couples once again polished off a couple of bottles of wine.

Carolyn woke the next morning with a hangover and tottered to the bathroom for an aspirin. When she returned she realized she had been sleeping next to the naked body of her best friend's husband. She dressed quietly and took a walk on the beach. The salty air cleared her head, and she made a decision.

At lunch that day she forced herself to bring up the subject. She admitted that she felt a terrible guilt about what had happened. All four friends agreed that the party was over—there would be no more swinging.

As soon as they returned home from the vacation, however, Chick began visiting Ginnie and Warren alone—and often until two or three in the morning. The fact that Carolyn could no longer arouse her husband's passion after his visits with the Longs confirmed her fears, and she hired me to document what she already knew to be true.

But I became more than a detective to Carolyn. Since she could no longer confide in her friend Ginnie, she poured out her feelings to me. Two or three times a week during the course of the investigation she showed up at my office in the late afternoon with a bottle of wine and sometimes a hunk of cheese. We got high as we discussed the problem of proving adultery in this bizarre case.

We knew we would have difficulty persuading a judge that Chick was balling his best friend's wife—with his blessing. The mere presence of the threesome in the same house late at night would not raise any judicial eyebrows. But bright street lights and an absence of shrubbery made it impossible to get close enough to the house to witness the orgies.

Meanwhile, Carolyn sank into depression. She found it difficult to concentrate on her work at the church and spent more time counseling with her boss than working for him. And she was turning me into a wino!

Chick might well have continued this devil's triangle indefinitely without getting caught. But he was eventually done in by Warren's job as a traveling salesman.

Warren was more than happy to share Ginnie's body—but only when he could witness the action. There was to be no sex between Chick and Ginnie when Warren was out of town. That would be cheating.

But Warren traveled often. Though Chick abided by the ground rules for several weeks, he soon began to take Ginnie out alone.

Several nights when Warren was out of town we followed Chick and Ginnie to clubs, watched them drink and dance, and then return to Ginnie's home. They spent hours there together with the lights out. Our evidence was building, but we still hoped to catch them in more intimate circumstances.

Then one evening I was preparing to enjoy a rare night at home with Shirley and the kids when my answering service relayed a message for me to call Carolyn. She told me she had followed Chick to the parking lot of the school where Ginnie taught. The two of them had met and driven off together in Chick's car. She wanted me to join her at the parking lot, where we would keep Ginnie's car under surveillance until the couple returned.

When I arrived at the school Carolyn joined me in my car. She had a paper bag in her hand. From it she removed a bottle of wine, glasses, a piece of cheese, a table knife and a box of crackers.

"Hi," she said, a little too brightly. "Her car is on the other side of the lot."

I moved my car over to get a better view of Ginnie's brown Pinto. Meanwhile, Carolyn opened the wine bottle and placed a large glassful into my hands. We settled down for the long wait.

"Listen, I've got some news," Carolyn said. "Chick's supposed to go to a convention next week in Philadelphia. I had a friend of mine check, and I found out that Ginnie is going out of town also."

I made a note of the date and location of the convention while Carolyn poured herself another glass of wine. She rested her head on the back of the seat and sighed.

"Boy, will I be glad when this whole mess is over," she said. "I've been so depressed . . . so lonely."

Tears came welling out of her eyes. She laid her head on my shoulder and sobbed for several minutes. Then she regained her composure and apologized. She was quiet for a minute while she retouched her makeup and ran a brush through her hair. I sipped my wine slowly, hoping that Chick and Ginnie would arrive soon to end this embarrassing scene.

"There, that's better," Carolyn announced, checking her face in a pocket mirror. "I'll try to cheer up and be a better date for you. Here, have some more wine." As she refilled my glass she rested her hand lightly on my leg.

I decided to bring the topic back to business and I asked her more details of the convention in Philadelphia the following week. It seemed like the perfect situation for us to gather the final evidence we needed.

"Oh, I don't want to talk about Chick anymore," Carolyn said thickly. "Let's talk about us."

"What about us?"

"You know . . . us!"

Carolyn slid over next to me and brought her lips up to my face. I could feel the pressure of her breasts against my arm. Suddenly she opened her blouse. She grabbed my hand and pressed it against her chest.

My mind said, "This is the worst possible thing for a private detective to do." But my body said, "Right on, sister!"

Suddenly I saw the glare of automobile headlights. I glanced up to see Chick's car pulling into the parking lot.

"Oh my God!" Carolyn whispered, and frantically buttoned her blouse. She slid down low in the seat.

Luckily for us, Chick and Ginnie were too involved with their own adultery to look across the parking lot. They sat there for ten minutes or so, kissing goodnight. As soon as they drove off in their separate cars Carolyn raced to her car and zoomed away.

The very next afternoon Carolyn showed up at my office with a bottle of wine.

"I just wanted you to know how much I enjoyed being with you last night," she said.

Professional sobriety had taken over.

"Carolyn, you're a beautiful woman," I said. "I sure don't blame you for being horny, but it would just be a horrible breach of ethics for me to make love to a client. I'd like to continue to be your friend as well as handle the investigation for you. But that's all I'm going to handle. Understand?"

Carolyn was quiet for a moment. "I understand," she said finally, a twinkle in her eye. "You can't blame me for trying, though."

"No, I can't. As far as I'm concerned you have every right to play around. But do me one favor: don't get caught," I said.

"Okay," she assured me.

It was the last time she brought wine to the office. We continued to be friends, but she never made another pass at me.

Meanwhile, I made plans to investigate Chick and Ginnie at the convention the following week. They were going to leave on a Tuesday and stay until Thursday. I was needed for another case all Monday night, and I wanted to get some sleep Tuesday morning, so I asked Jim Trexler and Linda Goodwin to set up the surveillance at the convention hotel. I planned to drive up Tuesday evening and join them for the remainder of the convention.

They followed the couple to Philadelphia without incident. The adulterers registered into adjoining rooms. Jim and Linda bribed the desk clerk to get a room just down the hall.

Before I left for Philadelphia I checked with my office.

Carolyn had left an urgent message for me to call her at work.

So I dialed her office at the church and heard Carolyn answer. She was glad to hear my voice, and she spoke in a conspiratorial tone.

"Remember you said it was okay if I played around, as long as I was careful?" she asked. "Well, I've got a big favor to ask of you. I'm going to a motel with someone this afternoon. Could you park outside and make sure we're not being followed when we go in?"

"Sure." I laughed.

She gave me the address of the motel and told me the encounter was set for 4 P.M.

"Want to know who?" she asked.

"Who?"

She giggled. "My boss!"

At 4 P.M. I watched as the minister drove to the motel and went to the reservation desk. He emerged a few moments later and walked casually to a room. In about ten minutes Carolyn drove slowly past my car. I nodded to her, indicating that everything was clear. She got out of her car and carried a brown-paper bag—presumably wine and cheese—into the motel room.

Leaving the couple to their pleasure, I drove toward Philadelphia. When Jim and Linda explained that the couple had registered in adjoining rooms, I was worried. If they each entered their own rooms, met through a connecting door, and left from their separate rooms in the morning we could not prove the adultery. Smart adulterers *always* take such precautions.

That evening Chick and Ginnie drank and danced for hours in the hotel's cocktail lounge. Jim and I took turns dancing with Linda. When Chick got ready to pay his check I sent Jim and Linda on up to our room. I lagged behind and hopped into the same elevator as our subjects. We would all watch carefully, hoping to witness Chick and Ginnie entering the same room.

They walked down the hall hand in hand, parted and entered separate rooms.

Morning came. We were sure the couple had slept together, but if they were as careful as they had been the night before we would not be able to prove a thing. About 8 A.M. we heard a chain rattle and Chick's door swung open. He walked into the hallway, and to our delight Ginnie came out after him, clasped his hand and walked down the hall with him!

During the rest of their stay the couple repeated the scene. Cautious at night but stupid in the morning, they allowed us to document their impropriety on Super-8 movie film.

Carolyn filed for divorce soon thereafter. When Warren heard at a preliminary hearing how he had been cheated, he filed for divorce himself, the victim of a lopsided triangle.

The last I heard, Carolyn was still working for the Protestant minister. She is remarried now. Her new husband is a traveling salesman.

18.

A PURSEFUL OF NAPKINS

"If you can play around, so can I," yelled Norma Jordan, whereupon her husband Randy gave her a backhand slap across the face. He stormed out of the house and was gone all night.

The very next day Norma hired me to investigate. I pocketed the large retainer she had drawn from her private savings account and agreed to begin surveillance later in the week.

But before I could start Norma had returned to my office to call me off the case. Randy had come home the night before and tearfully apologized for striking her. He said he loved her, but found it difficult to remain faithful to one woman. Even though he realized the unfairness of a double standard, he could not bear the thought of Norma playing around behind his back.

"He brought home this magazine," Norma said, and showed me a thick catalog published by a club in New Jersey.

I thumbed through it. It was filled with what appeared to be classified ads printed under photographs. I read one of them: "Happily married couple looking for attractive young female for threesome. Wife AC-DC." Then there was a registration number.

Norma was very excited. "Randy said that if we joined this club and played around *together*, he would agree to give up his girlfriend. Last night we sent off the application form!"

I wished Norma luck and began to return her retainer, but she stopped me.

"Keep it for now," she said. "Maybe this won't work."

I wondered if this swinging arrangement would save the marriage, and I made Norma promise to keep me informed. Over the next few months she discussed the situation with me frequently.

Every day for a week Randy rushed home early from work. He eagerly checked the mail to see if any word had arrived. Finally they were able to make a contact through the club. They had already leafed through the catalog many times and had decided to answer one ad in particular. It was placed by a "happily married" couple from Roanoke, Virginia. From their photograph they appeared to be in their early forties, close to the Jordans' age.

The procedure was simple but secretive. Randy and Norma composed a brief letter stating that they were interested in learning more about swinging. They enclosed a photograph. They then sealed their letter and wrote the registration number of the Roanoke couple on the outside. They placed that sealed envelope in another one, along with a small fee, and mailed it to the club, which forwarded the letter to the Roanoke couple.

Within a week a reply arrived.

The couple were coming to Washington on a Tuesday night. Could they drop in and meet Randy and Norma?

Could they ever!

Norma spent all weekend shopping for the right dress, but she could not decide how much cleavage to reveal. Finally she chose a cranberry-colored one that had buttons from neck to navel. She could button or unbutton her neckline depending upon her mood. Randy bought a mod suit with tight-fitting pants and open-neck collar.

On Tuesday Norma fiddled with her neckline as she prepared a plate of hors d'oeuvres. Finally the doorbell rang. Randy rushed to answer it while Norma impulsively tore two more buttons open. In an instant the fledgling swingers realized the Roanoke couple had used a very old photograph. They were at least in their mid-fifties. As they strode confidently into the house Norma quickly turned to button up her dress.

She could see that Randy was fuming over the couple's deception. There was to be no swinging that night.

But in spite of the disappointment the four spent a rather enjoyable evening discussing the subject of swinging. The Roanoke couple told them there was a special club in downtown Washington where swingers met other swingers on Saturday nights.

The older swingers also introduced Randy and Norma to some of the rules. The swingers club in downtown Washington was for "happily married" couples only. That meant that swapping partners was fine on occasions when everyone agreed, but there was to be no private hanky-panky when the party was over.

"Many of the women are AC-DC," the Roanoke woman said. "I am."

Norma was confused. "Does that mean you can't have babies?"

"No." The older woman giggled. "It means I enjoy sex with men *and* women."

"I love to watch her with another woman," her husband confided.

As they left, the couple invited Randy and Norma to meet them at the swingers' club the following Saturday evening.

Randy and Norma made fierce love to one another that night. Though disappointed with their first contact, they decided to visit the club in hopes of finding a couple nearer their own age.

On Saturday night they drove downtown, to an old, sleazy bar on a main street in Washington. On Saturday night the back room of the bar is taken over by the swingers of the nation's capital. Nervously Randy and Norma approached the man guarding the door and mentioned the first names of the Roanoke couple. That was their passport inside.

The noisy, smoke-filled room was packed with couples ranging in age from thirty to sixty. Nine out of ten women were dressed in flimsy, filmy fashions purchased at Frederick's of Hollywood.

Randy and Norma did not see the Roanoke couple, but they were immediately greeted by several others who were more to their liking. During the next two hours they exchanged first names and phone numbers with a half-dozen other couples.

There was one couple they found particularly attentive. Randy was turned on by the auburn-haired wife, who was wearing a see-through harem-girl outfit. Norma could not take her eyes off the slim hips of the woman's husband. They arranged to have dinner together the following week.

They drove home with their hands all over one another and rushed to the bedroom. Norma told me later that it was undoubtedly the best sex they had ever had together.

Norma came to visit me once or twice a week while all this was taking place. I tried to return her money, but I could see that she was still afraid. She was too turned on to turn back, but she worried that Randy might find a woman he liked better than her.

If only they would stick to the ground rules, I assured her, it would work.

She seemed hopeful. Randy was coming home eagerly and making frequent love to her. He had stopped running around entirely.

Dinner with the other couple went well. They all decided to spend the following weekend together at a fancy, secluded motel in the mountains.

This time Norma had little difficulty in choosing a wardrobe. She found a Frederick's of Hollywood store and bought several sexy dresses and nightgowns. On Saturday evening they all met at the motel and shared a quiet dinner that crackled with enjoyable tension. All of them were eagerly awaiting dessert!

They adjourned to the cocktail lounge, where they drank and danced for several hours. Norma enjoyed dancing with the other man, but she could feel her nervousness growing. The other couple were well aware that Randy and Norma were beginners, so they let nature and liquor take their course.

At 2 A.M. the lounge closed and the foursome piled into one motel room to continue the party. Randy found some music on the radio and danced with Norma. They slipped their shoes off. The men removed their shirts. Suddenly Norma was dancing with the other man ... then she was dancing with the other woman. Randy eased his wife onto the bed and stripped off her thin gown. He entered her. Next to them on the same bed the other couple began to make love. Casually the other woman slipped her hand onto Norma's breast. Her husband moved back as the woman kissed Norma. Randy, too, watched as the woman buried her face in Norma's crotch. Drunk and disorderly, Norma smiled up at her husband and saw him grinning in approval. The other woman turned her body around in the "69" position and Norma discovered that she was, indeed, AC-DC.

Then, in Norma's own words, "They all began to work on me. We must have looked like a can of worms on the bed together. I never had so many orgasms in my life."

Norma woke up the next morning to find herself in bed with three other naked people. She looked up at Randy and he grinned at her. They drove home that day bubbling over with excitement.

By this time Norma was convinced that swinging would save her marriage. She finally agreed to take her retainer back.

"But there's one condition," I told her.

"What?"

"That you get me into the club."

Norma grinned. "Sure."

We made a date for Saturday night. I wanted to show Shirley the scene, but to get her there I told a little white lie. I said I was investigating a couple that would be at a very unusual club. I bought her a low-cut minidress for the occasion.

On the way downtown I explained more about the club to Shirley. She seemed a bit dubious but agreed to go along with the ploy. If anyone asked, I worked as a sales manager and we had been swinging for one year.

I told the doorman that we were supposed to meet Randy and Norma, and he stepped aside to let us enter. Shirley's eyes bugged out (so did mine!) at the amount of skin being displayed. To her credit, she shoved her own ample chest forward and marched into the room. I followed stiffly behind her.

We were immediately surprised by the caliber of the people. I recognized several attorneys, an official of the U.S. Department of Health, Education and Welfare, the administrative aide to a U.S. senator, a doctor and a television newsman. All are prominent in Washington society, and all were accompanied by their wives. Another couple came up to us and started a conversation. The woman asked Shirley, "How long have you been . . ."

". . . a year!" Shirley stammered nervously.

"Are you AC-DC?"

". . . uh . . . sometimes!"

But Shirley soon overcame her nervousness and played the role of the swinging sales manager's wife. Couples kept writing their first names and phone numbers onto napkins and stuffing them into her purse.

"Across the room," I whispered to her, and indicated Randy and Norma. "They're the ones we're supposed to meet."

We worked our way across the room as Shirley gathered

more names and phone numbers in her purse. I could tell she was enjoying herself. The club was a place where married men and women could openly flirt with one another. It was, frankly, refreshing.

Finally we were next to Randy and Norma. Randy looked hungrily up and down Shirley's body, I returned the compliment to Norma. We had a couple of drinks and talked. Norma winked at me, wrote down her phone number and gave it to Shirley.

After a couple of hours we turned to leave. Shirley excused herself first to go to the bathroom. She returned with an amazed look on her face.

"There are two women in there kissing!" she said.

As we left I explained to Shirley that Randy and Norma had appeared to be heading toward a divorce. Shirley was amazed.

"They seem so happy," she said.

And indeed they do. Randy and Norma are still together, and still swinging. It saved their marriage.

I would not hesitate to recommend the same solution to other couples who are having similar difficulties. There is a certain type of person who seems psychologically driven to adultery. He or she can be happily married and still feel a deep need to hop in bed with a stranger. It seems to me that such a person is far better off committing adultery with the approval of his or her spouse than having a secretive affair—providing, of course, that both husband and wife can handle the emotional aspects of swinging.

You may be wondering what Shirley and I did with that purseful of napkins containing all those first names and phone numbers.

Shirley made me promise not to tell!

19

COMFORTING THE WIDOW

I would like the public and my clients to think that I am as invincible as the fictional private detectives on the TV screens. Regrettably, I have an ass like anyone else, and I occasionally fall on it with a very painful thud.

My Southern Baptist upbringing compels me to tell the truth—on occasion, I have been had. The following three stories are about adulterers who are still smiling.

An old black woman walked into my office one morning carrying a brown paper bag. My secretary assumed she was a cleaning lady who had brought her lunch, but the woman asked if she could see me.

She said she was a cook in a government cafeteria. "Mr. Pearce, I don't make much money. How much will this cost?"

"I'm afraid that the very minimum charge would be $10 per hour plus all expenses. And we require a retainer of no less than $300 before we can begin. Is this going to be a problem?"

To my surprise she replied, "No, I can pay you tomorrow."

Before we were finished she paid me $800. I cut corners for her whenever I could, but the woman drained her entire life's savings in order to pay for the investigation. And as I proceeded with the case I realized that she was really trying to protect her adulterous husband.

Bertha Walters had been married to Lawrence for more than thirty years. She said they had been very happy until about a year earlier, when she noticed his sexual appetite had waned. At first she attributed it to the onset of old age (a rationalization, by the way, which I hear very frequently as a coverup for adultery).

"What is your husband's occupation?" I asked.

"He's a Baptist minister."

"What makes you suspect that he's having an affair?"

"Well, lots of times he doesn't come home until seven or eight or nine o'clock at night."

"Isn't that normal for a minister?"

"He used to come home earlier."

"Is there any other reason for your suspicions?"

"Yes. I found . . . I found lipstick on his shorts."

I was sure her imagination was running wild.

"Are you positive?" I asked.

Silently she reached into the brown-paper bag and removed a pair of blue-and-white-striped boxer shorts. On the side was a large unmistakable stain of fire-engine-red lipstick.

"Could it possibly be yours?"

She answered me with a cold stare. "No!"

The she dumped a half-dozen pairs of shorts onto my desk. All showed the same brilliant red lipstick. I packed the laundry back into the bag and told her I would keep it for evidence.

The next day she gave me a photograph of her husband. Lawrence was old and very skinny and wore thick dark glasses.

A minister, oddly enough, is very tough to follow. He has no set schedule and flits from one address to another all day long. I would have preferred to use two cars, but I did not want to run up a big bill.

Though I was only charging Bertha for my own time, I brought along a new assistant, whom I will call Roland Davis. A retired military man, he had recently come to me for a job in order to relieve the boredom of sitting around home. This case seemed like a good one on which to break him in.

The two of us staked out Lawrence Walters' apartment on a Monday morning. It was a humble brick building in northwest Washington. He left home about 11 A.M. in a tiny foreign economy car. From the beginning it was obvious that one surveillance car would be sufficient, for he drove in a lazy, unconcerned manner. Even when changing lanes he never bothered to check his rear-view mirror.

The Reverend made short visits that day to a couple of hospitals and several private homes. Each time he stopped I called his wife and told her where he was. Each address proved to be a routine stop on his itinerary, and he remained only briefly inside each home.

Tuesday was a dull carbon copy of Monday—after two boring days we had no indication as to the source of the bright red lipstick.

We picked up the surveillance again on Thursday morning. Roland and I arrived about 9 A.M., just in time to see our subject's car pulling away from the curb and heading in our direction. I had to do a quick U-turn to stay with him.

This time the Reverend headed his car out of town. He drove many poky miles to Waldorf, Maryland, and then turned off onto a dirt country lane outside of town. He parked next to a modest home—"Franklin" was painted on the mailbox.

Lawrence walked inside without bothering to knock.

I placed a call to Mrs. Walters at the cafeteria, and she told me that several church members lived in Waldorf.

"Right now he's at the Franklins' house," I told her.

"Mrs. Franklin sings in the choir," she said.

"Is she sick?"

"No."

"Did Mr. and Mrs. Franklin show up for prayer meeting last night?"

"She was at church last night. There is no Mr. Franklin. He died about a year ago."

Why was Lawrence visiting the woman early in the morning if he had seen her at prayer meeting only the night before? I wanted to catch a good glimpse of the color of Mrs. Franklin's lipstick.

When we returned to the house Lawrence was still inside. We found a parking place down the road where we could watch his car, but the house itself was in an open area that precluded us from sneaking up on it.

Mrs. Franklin must have needed a lot of comforting, for the Reverend spent four hours inside. When he left, there was still no sight of the widow. In spite of the fact that other church members lived this far out in the country, Lawrence drove straight back to town.

Friday proved to be another routine day. The trip to Mrs. Franklin's house, therefore, was the only suspicious activity during the whole week.

The next morning Roland picked me up in his car, and we drove to Washington to continue the surveillance.

The Reverend led us right back out to Waldorf to the home of Mrs. Franklin. This time he only remained inside for an hour. We followed him to a grocery store, where he purchased a bag of food, and then he went right back to Mrs. Franklin's home! Once again he stayed for about four hours. We still saw no sign of the widow.

Proving adultery to the satisfaction of the court would be almost impossible if Lawrence confined his activities to this quiet country home. There was no way to peer inside the windows without alarming the neighbors, so we were forced to remain in our car down the street. And Lawrence had an ace in the hole—since Mrs. Franklin was a church member he had every reason to visit her. Yet all my instincts told me that Lawrence was not giving Bible studies in that house all day.

I had to see the mysterious Mrs. Franklin. So without

telling my client (and without charging her) I staked out the church the next morning. It was a warm summer day, and the church windows were wide open. The choir bellowed out "The Old Rugged Cross," and I wondered which voice belonged to Mrs. Franklin.

"Brothers and Sisters," a deep voice boomed, "my heart fills with joy to see all of you here today to worship the Lord."

A chorus of fervent "Amens" roared through the church.

Reverend Walters proved to be considerably more long-winded than my old preacher back in North Carolina. He denounced the devil for a full two hours before sitting down on his lipstick-decorated shorts. Two hymns and a prayer later, the service ended.

I was parked across the street from Mrs. Franklin's car as a mob of people filed slowly out of the church, stopping to pump the Reverend's hand. Bertha stood proudly at his side. The last person out of the church stopped for a long chat with the minister and his wife. She was an attractive black woman about forty or forty-five years old, built like a brick temple.

I thought she would never stop gabbing, but finally she walked toward her car. I pulled my own car out onto the street and eased slowly past as she approached. She nodded a Christian greeting to me and smiled. Her lips were caked with bright fire-engine-red lipstick—a fact that must have been painfully obvious to poor Bertha.

Monday morning I called my client. "I'm not suggesting anything," I said, "but is it usual for him to make two long visits to Mrs. Franklin?"

"Well, he does visit her."

"Look, I didn't charge you for it, but I stopped by the church yesterday so I could get a good look at her—"

"Oh, where were you? I didn't see you. I'm so sorry. Why didn't you come over and say hello?"

I explained that I had not come inside. "Are you still checking his shorts?" I asked.

"Yes. I haven't found any more lipstick."

Lawrence behaved himself until Wednedsay, when he once again headed for Waldorf. I dropped Roland off in a clump of trees to watch the house while I drove to a phone to call the client.

"Is Mrs. Franklin sick?" I asked.

"I don't think so."

"Is she going to be at prayer meeting tonight?"

"Oh, yes. I'm going to meet with her to discuss a special Sunday-school class."

"Well, look. We're down here in Waldorf. He's here."

There was a moment of silence. Then a soft, "Oh!"

Lawrence had no business at Mrs. Franklin's home that day. He would see her that night at prayer meeting, and the long drive to Waldorf was a waste of the church's mileage budget.

But how could we *prove* anything?

Looking back on the case, I'm sure that Bertha never wanted a divorce. Perhaps she merely wanted to confront her husband with the evidence, plead with him to change his ways and prevent a church scandal.

Bertha told me quietly that she had decided to drop the case. I offered to follow her husband a few more times for free, but I doubted that Lawrence would ever give us sufficient evidence.

"It's not the money," Bertha assured me. "I just can't go on with this anymore. Anyway, I think Lawrence is getting suspicious."

"Why?"

"He asked me what happened to all his shorts."

I had the shorts, but I didn't have a case against the Reverend.

20

THE INSIDE MAN

This is the most infuriating case I ever had. I'm embarrassed as I recall the details. My only defense is that it came early in my career, and it taught me a lesson that I guess I had to learn—once.

It will never happen again.

A woman by the name of Susan Smith called me one day and asked me to meet her at a restaurant in southern Maryland. When we were seated at a table she explained that she wanted me to investigate her husband, Danny, because she planned to divorce him in six months. Surprised, I asked why she did not want an immediate divorce. She explained that she and her husband owned a large tobacco farm, and she was not about to let a divorce interfere with business. Though Susan handled most of the farm planning and management, Danny's physical strength was a necessary part of bringing in the valuable harvest. Only when the crop was in could she afford to divorce her husband.

All of this presented a problem. Once I determine and officially inform a client that his or her spouse is committing adultery, the client must immediately stop sleeping with the spouse. If I proved adultery on Danny and Susan continued to sleep with him, she would be legally condoning his unfaithfulness. Even one quick round in bed with her husband would totally negate the entire investigation, and we would be forced to start again from scratch to make a case.

"Don't tell me officially," Susan suggested. "Just keep the reports in your files until my lawyer asks for them. Be careful, though. Danny has a lot of friends around here. If they find out what you are trying to do they will make it rough on you."

Susan agreed to help me by alerting me whenever Danny planned to be away from home for any extended period.

Thirty-two-year-old Danny Smith is a swaggering, beer-drinking, man-about-small-town. His reputation as a lover is very important to him, and he likes to brag loud and long about his women as he sits around the country taverns.

(Susan, by the way, was far more discreet. Her boyfriend was the owner of one of those taverns, but they only met under carefully guarded conditions.)

It seems that every country boy I follow is a maniac on the road. Danny raced his pickup truck along the flat, straight roads with total disregard for his own safety. Jim Trexler and I had to take the surveillance a step at a time, following him only short distances and gradually building a pattern of his activities. He often stopped at various country bars, but they seemed to be frequented only by regular customers, and I did not want to make myself conspicuous by following him inside.

After several weeks of occasional surveillance we followed him to the Capitol Beltway. The highway is heavily patrolled by police cruisers so Danny was forced to drive more sanely. Using two cars we pursued him to Alexandria, Virginia.

My heart thumped as he stopped his truck directly across the street from my office! *Had he discovered me?*

Jim and I watched nervously as Danny eased out of his truck, walked across the street toward my office building, and then proceeded to a small apartment a few blocks away. Two very relieved detectives followed him there.

We could not see which apartment he entered, but we

checked the names on the mailboxes. I called Susan and read the names to her, but none of them were familiar. Danny stayed inside for four hours, and when he emerged we were able to spot the downstairs apartment he had visited. The name on the door was Thomas.

Back in the office I shuffled papers for a few hours and then walked back and pounded on the door of the Thomas apartment. A petite woman about twenty-five years old answered. Her long black hair fell to her waist. A little girl toddled about at her feet.

"Is this the resident manager's apartment?" I asked.

"No. He's in apartment three."

I ran a credit check on Mrs. Thomas and discovered that her husband had deserted her shortly after the birth of their child. Her first name was Alicia. She was living on welfare, but her apartment had not appeared to be that of a destitute woman.

The following week Danny arranged a very careless date. We followed him to a motel only a few miles away from his farm. He entered the restaurant, and through binoculars we could see that Alicia and her daughter were already waiting inside. The three had lunch together, and several of Danny's boisterous friends dropped by the table to chat. He was showing off his latest conquest.

After lunch Danny ordered dessert—in one of the motel rooms. He spent the entire afternoon there along with Alicia and her daughter. We took photographs of the three of them coming out of the room together.

The case seemed almost too easy!

I told Susan, unofficially, that we had compiled sufficient evidence. But I asked her to continue to call me whenever Danny remained away from home so that I could spot check Alicia's apartment down the street from my office.

My surveillance reports, including the motel photographs, were carefully stored in the Smith file locked in my desk drawer. From time to time Susan called, and I would walk over to Alicia's apartment and wait for Danny to appear. Sometimes he did, and I taped the door; sometimes he did not. The file gradually became thick with incriminating evidence.

As instructed, I kept the file while Susan awaited the tobacco harvest.

Exhausted from too many days and nights of work, I took a few days off at that point for a vacation at Nag's Head, North Carolina, with Shirley and the kids. When I returned to my office my secretary informed me that a man named Roland Davis had been calling persistently about a job. I interviewed him, liked him and immediately put him to work on the Walters case, as reported in the preceding chapter.

The two of us kept very busy over the next few months. Roland seemed to do his work well, and I relied on him more and more. He virtually ran the office when I was gone, and he was competent enough to handle various investigatory tasks by himself.

One morning Susan Smith called and explained that Danny had been gone all night. Roland was not in the office at the moment, or I would probably have sent him over to watch Alicia's apartment. Instead, I walked over by myself. I could hear muffled voices inside the apartment as I cautiously inserted the matchstick in the door.

I was walking to a good vantage point about a half block away when I suddenly stopped in amazement. There was Roland's car in the parking lot. What was he doing here?

I settled down to wait for Danny to emerge from his lover's apartment, but I kept a close watch on Roland's car. After about forty-five minutes Alicia's door opened and she walked out hand in hand—not with Danny, but with Roland! I scooted for cover behind some bushes and watched in disbelief as the two of them walked to Roland's car and kissed goodbye. My assistant drove off, leaving his confused and stunned boss watching from the bushes.

This may have been the precise moment when my ulcer first made its presence known. Back in my office I stormed around, holding my stomach, and trying to figure out Roland's game. I checked the Smith file, but it was still intact. Angrily I grabbed a telephone tap, hooked it up to my very own phone, and concealed it in a closet.

Roland arrived at the office about 2 P.M. Trying to seem composed, I told him I would be gone for a few hours. For the rest of the afternoon I kept my own office building under surveillance.

When I returned Roland was ready for the night's work. It was difficult to hold a stakeout with him that evening, but I could not afford to alarm him until I figured out what he was doing. After a long night of surveillance I rushed back to my office, clutching my stomach, and played the taped messages from the previous afternoon. I heard Roland call his wife and sweet-talk her into believing that he had been on an investigation with me the night before, when he really had been with his girlfriend!

Then the bastard called Alicia. Right there on my office phone they had a fight. Roland told her he had picked the lock on my desk and had checked the names on all my files. But since the files were listed in my client's names he could not discover the folder that had the reports on Alicia. It was apparent that Roland had been seeing Alicia for a long time and had noticed me hanging around her apartment taping the door. Afraid that his own name might be dragged into court, he applied for a job with me!

Roland demanded that Alicia reveal the name of her other lover. She denied having one. Roland finally roared, "I'm coming right over and beat the shit out of you until you tell me his name!"

"Okay," Alicia sobbed. "You win. It's Danny. Danny Smith." The call ended abruptly.

Apprehensively I opened my desk drawer. The Smith file had vanished.

I called Roland's home. He had not yet arrived. I told his wife I wanted to see him right away. Then I hung up and nursed my ulcer.

Roland showed up in a few hours. I stifled an impulse to throw him out the window and bluntly accused him of stealing the file.

He pleaded innocent. How could I possibly imagine such a thing? He was a loyal, dedicated employee. He would never pull a dirty trick like that. He finished up his speech with a weak attempt at a smile, and the sight of his phony grin pushed me over the brink.

"You lying son of a bitch!" I roared. "If I didn't have this phone tapped I'd probably believe your bullshit! I'd even probably believe that I didn't see you come out of that whore's apartment!"

A look of horror crossed his face, and he ran from the room. I haven't seen him since. I partially settled the score by scrawling an anonymous note to Roland's wife naming Alicia, giving her address, and spelling out certain dates and times when they had been together.

But despite my temporary satisfaction with that, I was the one who was scheduled for a long, slow trip to the ovens. The evidence that Susan had paid plenty for me to collect was probably destroyed by now, and she had no case.

There was one chance.

If Roland had not given the file to Alicia—and if Alicia had not alerted Danny—then we still might win in court. For there was one incriminating piece of evidence: the room-registration files of the small-town motel. Susan's lawyer could subpoena it as evidence to corroborate my verbal testimony. But it could not be subpoenaed until the divorce papers were served. If Danny was warned ahead of time he might be able to get the motel record destroyed. I could only sit and wait until the tobacco crop came in.

I called the police and reported the burglary of my office. Then I drank a glass of milk.

In a couple of weeks I received a call from Susan's attorney. He was ready to file suit for divorce, and he wanted the records of my investigation. "They were stolen," I sheepishly admitted.

The enraged attorney threatened to sue me. I took the verbal abuse, then I pointed out that the motel record might be enough to prove the case.

That very afternoon the attorney subpoenaed the motel record. It was missing.

Danny was one of the stupidest adulterers I have ever known, but he was by far the luckiest. Susan finally divorced him on grounds of mental cruelty, after an agonizing eighteen-month separation. Her settlement was far less than it should have been.

Roland, wherever you are, I owe you one!

However, two good things resulted from this wretched case. First, I learned that Scotch mixes well with milk. Second, I learned to trust no one with my records. I have a great group of assistants, and I often place my personal safety in their hands—but they will never touch my files. Now, after each night of surveillance, I immediately make copies of all the notes we have taken. The originals are then locked inside a vault at my home, not at my office. My home is guarded twenty-four hours a day by a sophisticated electronic alarm system that automatically dials the police. The house is never left unoccupied and, at any rate, almost no one knows where I really live. I maintain a legal residence in Alexandria, but my real home is many miles away.

And the copies of my files are kept in a vault at an entirely different location.

Not even Shirley knows where they are.

21

MR. EXCITEMENT

Louis Horton was so dull he was absolutely brilliant. For three months he played with his lover right under my nose, and I never had a clue. He was the cleverest adulterer I have ever chased.

When Louis's youngest child went off to college, he sat his wife down for a serious talk. He said he had been waiting for the day when all the children were grown up so he could end the thirty-one-year-old marriage.

Shocked, Margaret asked if he had a lover. No, he said without emotion, there was no other woman. He was merely tired of the marriage. He promised to continue making the mortgage and college-tuition payments, and he volunteered to give Margaret a substantial monthly check. He wrote down the address of an apartment in Falls Church, Virginia, told Margaret she could visit or call any time, and left.

Margaret was stunned. Still in love with her husband but dazed and wounded, she confided her plight to a co-worker at the bank where she had been employed for fifteen years. The friend happened to be an ex-client of mine and recommended that I look into the case.

Margaret appeared in my office about three weeks after Louis had moved out. Still uncertain as to what she wanted to do, she poured out her troubles. In her heart she did not believe there was another woman. Yet her mind kept telling her that, dull as he was on the outside, Louis had always been a tiger in bed. She could not imagine his living alone—sleeping alone—for very long. As we talked she came to a decision. If Louis was still faithful to her, she would continue to hope for his return. But if he was in love with another woman, she wanted a quick divorce.

There was only one way to find out.

Since I had come highly recommended, Margaret did not hesitate to write me a check for $1,000. My previous experience investigating newly separated husbands led me to believe that the case would be a quick one. I figured I would have to refund part of her money.

The apartment that Louis had rented was out of character with his $25,000-a-year job. The old, rundown three-story brick building contained two apartments on each floor, and rented mainly to lower-income families. But, since Louis was still supporting Margaret in style, I could understand why he had been forced to move to this ramshackle neighborhood.

Jim Trexler and I arrived at the apartment about 5 P.M. one day and copied down the names on the mailboxes. I called Margaret, but she failed to recognize any of the names. I placed the list in my files for future reference.

Louis arrived home about six o'clock, dressed in his normal workaday attire of a dark suit, white shirt and modest striped tie. When he entered his apartment we taped the door. His blinds were pulled and the windows covered with thick, heavy drapes, so it was impossible to see inside the apartment.

We dutifully checked the tape about every half hour, and it remained undisturbed. From our car we could watch anyone enter or leave the building. An unattractive woman arrived about 6:30 and entered the first-floor apartment adjacent to Louis's. Later an older couple left a third-floor apartment to walk their dog. These fascinating moments were the *only* activity of the evening. Louis remained inside his apartment, not even bothering to pick up his newspaper from the hallway. As we periodically checked the tape we could hear the television blaring.

The lights in his apartment went out around 11 P.M. We waited until midnight, finally yawned at one another and drove home.

This exciting routine was repeated every night that week. Jim suggested that we charge time-and-a-half for boredom.

Margaret was not at all surprised that her husband seemed to be behaving himself. She found it a little unusual that none of his old friends came to visit, but she was accustomed to Louis's dull life style. She seemed heartened by the lack of sexual evidence and continued to hope that Louis would return home.

Our next tactic was to watch him during the weekend, in case he came out of hibernation.

By 9 A.M. Saturday Jim and I were yawning outside his apartment. Louis left at 9:15 and drove to his former home, where he spent the morning mowing the lawn, repairing some window screens and puttering around in the garage. Then he got in his car and once again took refuge in the old brick building. Through his door we could hear the sounds of a football game on television. Margaret had mentioned that Louis was addicted to the sport.

In the middle of the afternoon he left the apartment, walked to a store, bought two six-packs of beer and returned home alone. He remained inside for the rest of the day, not even emptying his trash or washing his laundry in the utility room. Every time we checked the tape we could hear the roar of the football games on television.

This kind of surveillance is more exhausting than a chase. With nothing to do for hour after hour, Jim and I grew very sleepy and very bored.

We finally agreed to take turns visiting a nearby bar, but

one of us was constantly monitoring the inaction at the apartment. Nothing happened. Absolutely nothing.

Or so we thought!

On Sunday morning Mr. Excitement made his big move. He left the apartment at 8:45 and drove to church. After the service he returned to the apartment and spent the rest of the day watching football games.

Jim and I again killed the day by alternating between the apartment and the bar. I felt a twinge of guilt at spending so much time over a bottle of beer, but one of us was always watching the apartment.

On Monday I advised Margaret to drop the case: it was a waste of money. But she seemed troubled by two things in our reports. First, Louis never drank beer, so why had he bought some? Second, he was a compulsive cleaner. He would never allow garbage to remain in the apartment over the weekend. Margaret paid me another $1,000 and asked me to continue.

The second week was a carbon copy of the first. The only incident out of the routine occurred when a furniture van delivered two large bookcases to Louis's apartment. Margaret confirmed that Louis was a voracious reader.

Then one day Margaret's friend from the bank—the woman who had recommended me—called to ask how it was going. Naturally I declined to discuss it, but then my former client told me that Margaret suspected I was covering something up.

Despite Margaret's suspicions, I still couldn't persuade her to drop the case. I explained that we occasionally run up against a blank wall, and it's not our business to manufacture evidence.

What seemed to bother Margaret most was her memory of Louis's sex drive. She was sure that by now he would have returned to her bed or found another one. So she refused to give up.

We worked the dull case sporadically for three months,

eventually charging Margaret about $3,000. Mr. Excitement never varied his routine. To be extra sure he wasn't sneaking out, we tried using two tapes on his door, one high and one low. We moved our car closer, where we could watch the apartment door very carefully. We watched him at his office. Louis invariably behaved himself, coming right home from work and spending the night alone in the apartment.

Or so we thought!

Finally one afternoon Margaret confronted me in my office and asked, "Are you sure you haven't talked to my husband? Are you sure you haven't gotten a bigger fee from him than I paid you?"

That did it!

"You're badly mistaken," I said, allowing my temper to rise. "I told you in the beginning that we will collect any evidence that exists and give you a full report. And we have. We can't make things happen. We can't make Louis leave the apartment and go find another woman."

Later that week Margaret sent me a certified letter asking for a day-by-day accounting of my charges. I documented every hour and each expense. When I finished I realized we had undercharged Margaret slightly, and I pointed that out in my letter of reply.

I was really angry now. Just to be positive that there was still no case I sat outside Louis's apartment for four more nights. No one was paying me. His routine had not changed, and after four boring nights I could stand no more. I had other cases to work.

Three more months passed before I received a letter from an attorney. He said he had reviewed my reports and concluded that the surveillance was not properly handled. His client was convinced that her husband's sexual appetite had to be appeased. Therefore, he was convinced that I had fouled up. He demanded that I return Margaret's money.

I naturally refused.

Whereupon I was informed that I would be sued for $100,000.

I was not worried (well, not much). Jim could corroborate my story. And the attorney eventually backed down. I pride myself on the professional details of my reports, and there was no case against me.

As far as I was concerned I had not won, but neither had I lost. You can't prove adultery if there is no adultery. Mr. Excitement behaved himself during the entire course of our investigation, of that I was certain. I was still blissfully unaware that dull, quiet Louis had committed adultery virtually every night of our investigation.

A year after Louis moved out, Margaret obtained a divorce on grounds of desertion. The settlement was probably not much different than Margaret would have received for an adulterous divorce. By this time she had a boyfriend and was planning to remarry.

But a few weeks after the divorce Margaret called me and gave me a verbal kick in the balls.

"I thought you'd like to know that Louis has a girlfriend," she said tauntingly. "He's not hiding it now, but he told me they have been going together for more than a year . . . *before he left home!* Her name is Edith McMahon."

"No way," I said to myself, as I pulled the file on Mr. Excitement. I leafed through it looking for some reference to the name Edith McMahon.

To my utter horror the name was right there in our very first report. Edith McMahon was the plain-looking woman who lived next door to Louis! We had copied her name from the mailbox during our first surveillance, but we had never seen anything to arouse our suspicions of her.

Jim rushed into the office and we discussed the woman. We remembered her well. We had watched her movements just as we had watched everyone in the building. She had come and gone frequently, but she never went near Louis's apartment, and vice versa.

"He's got to be lying," I said to Jim. "He met her after the investigation."

We ran a credit check on Edith McMahon, and I learned that she worked in another government office a few blocks from Louis. I went to her office posing as a newspaper reporter in need of some information. She was very helpful, and I flirted with her.

"How about going to dinner with me tonight?" I asked.

She blushed. "Thanks, but I can't. I'm going to get married. I have been going with a man for more than a year."

I roared back into my office, slammed the door and sat in silence at my desk. Then I ordered my secretary to cancel a couple of appointments I had for the next day. Next I called a friend in the office of the real-estate company that rented Louis his apartment.

Early the next morning Jim Trexler, Linda Goodwin and I sat outside the building in three separate cars. Edith left her apartment about 7:30 A.M. and Linda followed her. A half hour later Louis left his apartment and Jim followed him. Nervously I listened to my two-way radio until both my assistants reported that the two people had arrived at their offices. I told them to sit tight and alert me if they left. Then I strapped on a walkie-talkie and moved into the building.

My friend in the realty office had provided me with a key, but he vowed to disown me if I was caught. I went in Louis's door.

Mr. Excitement kept a very neat apartment. The trash cans, as Margaret had predicted, were empty. In the bedroom closet, however, was an array of women's clothing as well as some of Louis's. I recognized the green dress I had seen Edith wearing the day before.

The puzzle was solved when I spotted a crack in the wall

just visible behind the bookcase. I discovered that a hole had been neatly cut behind it, big enough for a person to walk through. I pushed aside an identical bookcase—and walked into Edith's apartment.

What could I do? To reveal my discovery would mean opening myself up to a charge of breaking and entering. I was forced to keep Louis's clever secret.

I stood for a few moments staring at the hole in the wall. Then I turned and walked meekly out of the apartment.

22

CHARITY CASE

This is the story of the Big Lie. Eddie Duncan was caught red-handed and bare-assed making love to his secretary.

Yet because of the Big Lie he got away.

A tall, graying, sophisticated liar, Eddie is a top executive of one of the country's largest charities. He spends his days collecting huge donations from rich contributors all over the country. Trouble began in the Duncan home when Eddie also began to collect long brown hairs on his clothing. When his silver-haired wife, Marjorie, questioned him he theorized the hairs came from the secretaries at work, who hung their coats on the same rack. Marjorie pretended to believe this dubious explanation, but she quietly collected the hairs that she discovered on Eddie's coat, pants, shirts and even his underwear.

They filled a small plastic bag by the time she came to see me.

I explained, as I always do, that I would not report to her officially until I had completed the entire investigation. Once she knew the details of her husband's adultery she would be forced to make him leave home, or she would legally be condoning the adultery. Our evidence would be worthless.

I asked for several items, including a photograph of Eddie and a list of employees at his office. She copied their last year's Christmas card mailing list and brought it to me.

Jim Metz and I began the surveillance on a Wednesday

afternoon at Eddie's office. We arrived early, about 2:30, in order to have a chance to walk through the office and obtain a glimpse of Eddie and his co-workers. Often a quick look will provide a good indication of who is extra friendly with whom. But as I walked past Eddie's office on the second floor I saw him already preparing to leave. I hustled back out the door, alerted Jim over the two-way radio, and we prepared to follow.

Eddie drove his car through a thunderstorm to a high-rise apartment building in suburban Virginia. Leaving the car engine running, he scooted inside through the storm. I told Jim to stay with the car, and I ran in after our subject.

Since we had just begun the case I did not want to blow my cover, so I let Eddie have the elevator all to himself. As soon as the elevator door closed I raced for the stairwell, flew through the doorway, and ran up to the second floor, pausing only a moment to make sure the elevator had not stopped there. At the sixth floor I managed to spot Eddie disappearing around a corner of the hallway.

In less than thirty seconds Eddie reappeared with a beautiful young woman on his arm. She looked to be about twenty-five or thirty years old. Her most striking feature was her long brown hair.

As they pushed the call button for the elevator I raced back down the stairwell, arriving breathlessly on the first floor in time to see them walking out the front door. I pushed on the stairwell door to follow them and discovered that it was locked. I was trapped!

I pounded vainly on the door, then ran back up the stairs, desperately testing each door. There were eight floors in the building, and all eight doors were locked. I had been drenched in the rain, and I was now sweating profusely from running up and down the stairs. It was hot and airless in the stairwell, and for a moment I thought I might pass out. Finally I caught my breath, cursed, and trudged back down to the first floor.

Meanwhile, Jim was dutifully following the couple, all

the while trying to reach me on his car radio. He tracked them back to the charity office, where they entered separate doors. He sat in the parking lot and waited.

I stood at the first-floor door and waited.

The late afternoon brought scores of people swirling through the lobby, but I could get no one's attention. Not until 7 P.M did a young couple approach the door. I rapped my keys against the safety glass, and they looked over. I motioned to them, and the man pushed the door open.

"Unit one to unit two," I muttered disgustedly.

"Where the hell have you been?" Jim asked.

"I'll tell you later," I growled. "What's happening?"

"I'm back at the office building. His car has been sitting here all afternoon and evening, but the building looks deserted."

I called Marjorie, and to my surprise Eddie answered the phone. I hung up in confusion.

Jim, properly chagrined at losing the subject, joined me at the apartment building. Together we went inside and copied the names of all the tenants on the sixth floor. One of them, a girl named Valerie Taylor, was on Eddie's office Christmas-card list.

The next day Marjorie explained that Eddie's car had broken down at work and he had taken a cab home. Jim had been babysitting an empty building.

But everything worked out fine the second night. Eddie had told his wife that he had to attend a meeting and would not be home until midnight. By late afternoon Jim and I were staked out at the girl's apartment.

Leaving Jim outside with strict orders not to drive away without me, I walked inside the building and carefully placed heavy masking tape over the latches of the stairwell doors on the first and sixth floors—and the fourth floor for insurance. Then with a match I taped the door of Valerie's apartment and hustled back down to wait with Jim.

Jim reported that Eddie had already arrived and was

parking his car. So I raced back up the six floors and was in position to see him step off the elevator with a bottle of liquor in his hand. Huffing and puffing, I retaped Valerie's door after he entered.

They were inside together for about an hour. Then they left, holding hands, and drove to the Capitol Hill Theater, where they saw the notorious X-rated movie *Censorship in Denmark.* Not all the action was on the screen—our subjects were petting heavily during the entire movie.

When they finally returned to Valerie's apartment, Eddie remained inside for about two hours.

Early the next week Marjorie came to my office and asked me to tell her about the investigation. I reminded her that legally I could not do so, but she assured me that we could talk off the record. A client is naturally interested in our progress, so if I feel that he or she can keep a secret, I will talk unofficially. Marjorie did not seem surprised to hear about Valerie. When I finished reading the report she was silent for a few moments. Then she asked me to recommend a divorce attorney. I gave her three names to choose from.

Marjorie hired one of them, and the three of us discussed the case. The lawyer wanted one more good report, and we decided that the most logical time would be an upcoming national convention for the charity, which both Eddie and Valerie were scheduled to attend.

On the morning of the convention Jim and I followed Eddie to the office. Valerie arrived and unabashedly placed her own suitcase in Eddie's car. I followed them later to the plush convention motel in the mountains of central Pennsylvania. Jim Trexler and Linda Goodwin had already registered there. Jim took 16mm movies of Eddie and Valerie arriving together while my car pulled in behind them.

By the time Eddie walked into the lobby I was standing next to the desk. I watched him register as Mr. and Mrs.

Edward Duncan. About a half hour later I approached the desk clerk and introduced myself as a convention delegate from California. I told him that I would be going out a lot with my old friend Eddie Duncan, and I requested a room near to him and his wife. He handed me the key to a room two doors down from our subjects, and he scrawled my fictitious name onto a delegate's badge.

For the next three nights we documented their activities as the administrators of the famous charity spent their expense money liberally. Many of the other delegates were obviously "married" to their secretaries during the convention, and Eddie and Valerie played with them openly. Each morning we took movies of the two of them leaving their room together.

When we returned to Washington Marjorie wanted a full report. She had demonstrated that she was cool enough to handle the knowledge, so we told her all the details. She called her mother, whose blunt advice was "Kick the son of a bitch out!"

But Marjorie was not yet ready to kick. It is always difficult to break up a thirty-year-old marriage, and she wanted a week to think things over.

The following Saturday Marjorie called. She had mentioned to Eddie that she was driving to Richmond the following day with several girlfriends. Eddie had seemed suspiciously anxious for her to go.

"Can you watch him tomorrow?" Marjorie asked.

I explained that we were very busy on another case and that, at any rate, we already had sufficient evidence against Eddie. I advised her not to spend any more money on the investigation.

I was relaxing at home on Sunday night when my answering service reported that a hysterical woman named Marjorie wanted me to call her. When I called she begged me to come right over. Sobbing uncontrollably, in bits and pieces, she told me the story of her incredible day.

She had left that morning for Richmond but

immediately found it impossible to allow Eddie such a golden opportunity. She was still in love with the man and could not bear the thought of his making love to his secretary all day. She told her girlfriends that she felt ill and persuaded them to leave her at the drugstore in a shopping center about two blocks from her home. Within minutes she spotted Valerie driving past the shopping center in the direction of her home. She tried to call me, but my answering service could not reach me.

After waiting an hour Marjorie could bear the pressure no longer. She marched back home, quietly unlocked the front door and walked inside. In the living room she spotted Valerie's raincoat and shoes. She could hear giggles in the bedroom.

Marjorie sneaked to a hall closet, grabbed her camera and attached a flash cube. Silently she sneaked down the hallway toward the bedroom. As she passed the open door of the bathroom she noticed the girl's clothes stacked in a neat pile. Skirt, blouse, bra and panties were all there. Unable to resist this incriminating evidence, Marjorie aimed her camera and fired.

The flash cube made a *pop!* Marjorie turned quickly and snapped a second photo of the raincoat and shoes in the living room. Whirling back toward the bedroom she saw the frightened Valerie, nude, running desperately for her clothes in the bathroom. Firing fast, she snapped a photo of her husband's naked secretary.

Eddie had pushed a dresser against the bedroom door, but Marjorie's adrenalin provided a moment of superhuman strength. Fiercely she shoved the barricaded door open. She took several photos of her frantic husband as he scrambled into his clothes.

Valerie, white and sobbing, kept assuring Marjorie that nothing had happened. She had just come over to discuss some business, she lied, and they had begun fooling around.

"We were just dancing naked," she said. "Just teasing."

"There wasn't any music on," Marjorie snapped, and the girl was quiet.

Eddie sheepishly emerged from the bedroom, determined to lie his way out of the embarrassing situation.

"Come on out," he said to Valerie. "This can be explained."

Valerie emerged from the bathroom, and the three moved to the living room, where they engaged in a sometimes calm, sometimes heated discussion for about two hours.

Eddie: "We didn't do anything. You know I love you."

Valerie: "I was just dancing naked in the bedroom with your husband. We didn't do anything."

Marjorie: "Bullshit!"

To her credit, Marjorie kept her cool. She resisted the temptation to tell them about our investigation. She ordered Valerie to leave. Then she demanded that Eddie move out immediately. Finally left alone, she wavered between suicide and one last attempt to reach me, which fortunately was successful.

Calmed by a double dose of tranquilizers, Marjorie assured me she could make it through the night. She agreed to meet me in the morning at her attorney's office.

The lawyer warned Marjorie that Eddie might play dirty. His job was to sweet-talk people out of their money, and he just might try to con Marjorie out of an adultery case. The attorney explained, as I had, that if Marjorie welcomed Eddie back into bed, she would be legally condoning Eddie's adultery and so render worthless every bit of evidence we had worked so hard to obtain.

Marjorie said she understood.

But it is oh-so-difficult not to believe what we want to believe. Marjorie had been married for thirty years. She loved Eddie! The prospect of life without him seemed unbearably bleak.

It is wonderful when a loving couple decide to reconcile. Many marriages have survived when an adulterous spouse is caught, is repentant and renews his vows of love.

But Eddie was a hustler. The smooth-talking charity worker received very sound advice from his attorney. After several days of living alone, Marjorie was overjoyed when Eddie invited her out to dinner. They talked things over while sharing a bottle of wine. Eddie said he was truly sorry. He used the Big Lie—he told Marjorie he still loved her. He slept with Marjorie that night, and the next day he moved back home.

Beaming with joy, Marjorie came to my office the following week and asked for my reports.

"It was worth the money!" she assured me. "It brought everything out into the open. He still loves me!"

I crossed my fingers.

Six weeks later Marjorie called. She had gone away for one day, she said, and when she returned Eddie had moved out. She was so embarrassed that she waited three days before she called me.

"You were right," she admitted tearfully.

Marjorie had no money, and Eddie had been thoroughly warned of our investigation. It would be practically impossible to get evidence on him now. He had won.

Marjorie filed for divorce on grounds of desertion. After waiting a full year, she was granted the divorce. The property was divided evenly, and since the children were all grown, alimony was set at a very low figure. The settlement would have been far greater had our reports been admissible evidence.

Marjorie moved to a modest apartment and took a job as a clerk in a department store, a victim of the Big Lie.

23

HOW TO COMMIT ADULTERY WITHOUT GETTING CAUGHT

The next adulterer or adulteress I attempt to catch in the act just might be you. If given unlimited time and money, I would probably catch you no matter how careful you were. But if you have read these twenty-two case histories carefully you have learned that there are many precautions you can take. If you work hard at adultery you can make my ulcer act up and perhaps stall the case until your spouse runs out of patience and/or cash.

You have been reading about some of my more difficult cases—the exceptions. Most adultery is boringly easy to prove. It only seems fair, then, that I give you a sporting chance to benefit from the knowledge I have gained through ten years and five hundred cases. So here are my ten rules on how to commit adultery without getting caught. If followed faithfully they will give me—or any detective—a most difficult time.

1. *Handle the money in the family yourself.* Adultery is generally not free love. There are numerous payments for dinners, gifts, cab rides, hotel rooms, drinks and travel. The financial burden is usually greater on the man, but even the woman must expend a certain amount of money for babysitters, travel, clothes and time lost from work. If you are the only family member keeping track of income and expenses, then the added costs of adultery will be relatively easy to hide.

Payments, needless to say, should always be made in cash. Never, *never* use a credit card if there is any chance that the charge record will be seen by anyone else. I have known some adulterers who took the simple precaution of renting an inexpensive post-office box known only to them, and applying for a credit card at that address. Thus the credit-card bill was mailed to the secret address and only the adulterer saw it.

Cash payments would be simpler.

It is also important, if you are stepping out, to watch your spouse's expenditures. Periodically check to see if a large, unaccountable chunk of cash is missing from the checking account, savings account or other financial reserve. If your spouse has made such a payment in secret, it may well have been handed over to a divorce attorney or a private detective. The missing money is likely to be your first clue that you are under suspicion and, quite possibly, surveillance.

2. Never show affection to your lover in public. Men and women have many legitimate reasons for being together other than for sex. A boss may need to take his secretary to lunch to discuss business. A woman may wish to have dinner with a family friend to plan a surprise birthday party for her husband. You may someday be forced to invent a reason for a certain meeting on a certain night, and the judge will have difficulty believing that you were preparing next week's Sunday-school lesson if we have photographs of you kissing while parked at a stoplight.

Public signs of affection are a very necessary part of our cases, for they are usually the only physical contact that we actually witness.

Even minor courtesies can be damning. Courts have ruled that when a man opens a car door for a woman, seats her in a restaurant or lights her cigarette, he is showing a sign of affection—if he normally does *not* extend the same courtesies to his wife.

3. Remember to use a pay phone. Wiretapping is one of the

most important tools of the private detective. Just because it is against the law don't assume your spouse will forbid a detective to install a tap. You may never know of its existence—but don't spend the rest of your life wondering how the detective knew you were going to be at the convention with your lover.

A tapped conversation can't be used in court, but it hurts your chances of a good settlement more than you might guess. Your spouse will receive most of the adultery evidence secondhand, presented rather matter-of-factly by the detective. But if you have been careless enough to allow your love talk to be recorded, your spouse will be confronted with evidence that is extremely difficult to forgive and forget.

Right from the beginning of any extramarital affair you should establish an understanding that your lover is never to call you at home or at the office. Set up a code signal. If the lover *must* contact you in an emergency situation, have him or her call and pretend to be a long-distance operator asking for a fictitious person. You can inform the "operator" that she has the wrong number, hang up and call back from a pay phone. Since the telephone companies have begun to use both male and female operators, this ploy can work for anyone.

But even this tactic should be used sparingly. One of my most lucrative cases began when a husband heard his wife answer such a phone call and then quickly make up an obviously phony excuse to get out to a store (and a pay phone).

Long-distance calls should be made with extra care, for a record of them appears on the monthly phone bill. If you follow the first commandment and are responsible for the family finances, you can hide such calls (and check on those made by your spouse). One of the regular items we ask to see when beginning a case is the family phone bill. We sit down with the client to check all the long-distance calls and can often discover the existence of a lover just from them.

Office phones are safer, for they are far more difficult to

tap. Nevertheless, there is always a danger that a nosy employee might overhear your conversation. Nosy employees who gain a little privileged knowledge have a nasty habit of becoming dangerous employees.

Pay phones are usually accessible, impossible to tap unless the adulterer makes a habit of using the same one constantly, and are a bargain compared to the cost of a divorce.

4. Check the rear-view mirror frequently. Before you meet your lover, and again after you drive off together, always take a few minutes to determine whether or not you are being followed. From time to time look under the car to see if anyone has installed a beeper. Always check the red covers of your taillights to see if any holes have been punched in them. Then keep a sharp eye out behind you as you drive.

Whether in traffic or not, take simple precautions. Do not drive a direct route, but circle aimlessly for a few blocks and see if another car is taking the same route. Then drive to your destination along the least-traveled roads.

Risk a traffic ticket to keep from getting caught. Crash stoplights just as they are turning red. Run stop signs. Speed along so fast that you will know that anyone who is keeping up with you is following you. Then pull off the road and wait for traffic to pass.

And remember to look for two cars, not merely one. Most detectives drive bland-looking cars, generally Fords or Chevys, and they often sport telltale temporary antennas hooked to the driver's window.

If you suspect that you are being followed, do not meet with your lover. If you are already together, then drive to a public place, such as a well-lit restaurant, sit very obviously in the center of the room, show no public signs of affection, and figure out a logical reason for the meeting. Then take your lover home, leave immediately, go to your own home, tell your spouse whom you met with and why, and make particularly vigorous love.

5. Rent adjoining rooms. Adjoining rooms can still be

found—they seem to have come back into style with the modern motor hotels that dot the highways. It is easy enough to call the motel first and ask if it has adjoining rooms. Then reserve two of them, register for them separately, enter and leave them separately. Have a good time together after you open the common door.

The small extra expense of renting an additional room is nothing compared to the cost of a divorce.

6. Look for taped doors. As I have frequently mentioned, our "tape" is a matchstick, bent in two and inserted on the hinged side of the door. When the door is opened the matchstick falls to the ground, telegraphing the fact that someone entered or left. Develop the habit of checking the doors for the telltale matchsticks, paying special attention to the hinged side, down low.

As soon as you enter, take a few moments to stand silently next to the door and listen for someone approaching. If the room has a peephole, watch. If you hear suspicious sounds open the door quickly. If a man in the hall suddenly drops to the floor to tie his shoelaces, you are under surveillance.

When you leave the room, check immediately for a bent matchstick on the floor. There will be only one, for the detective will quickly remove used ones.

7. Do not turn off the lights. You can invent all sorts of plausible excuses for spending time together with a member of the opposite sex—if the lights are on. But if all the lights are turned off there can only be one logical explanation, and it often results in a bitter and costly court battle. So, when you enter a room, an apartment or a house, turn on a variety of lights. And leave them on.

I know, I know! Many lovers object to sex with the lights on. But this can be handled simply and sensibly. Leave the lights *on* in the living room and *off* in the bedroom.

8. Shower after sex. Two or more naked people writhing about on a bed create a variety of exciting but very suspicious odors. So always shower after adulterous sex, but don't rush home with your hair all wet and messed. Don't use soap, for it will telegraph its own perfumed scent. Coming home having obviously showered is like wearing a sign around your neck saying, "I just had sex."

Simply take a quick, water-only shower to wash away the odors and check your clothes carefully for hair, lipstick, perfume and any other suspicious substance.

9. Involve other people. Unless a detective witnesses the actual sex act he will have difficulty proving adultery if more than two people are involved. If you are with your lover and you suddenly suspect that you are under surveillance, immediately call a trusted friend and have him or her join you. The three of you should invent a legitimate reason for being together. Then leave with your friend, not with your lover.

If you are discreet you might be able to pair up with another couple. Have the two men rent a hotel room, and the two women rent the adjoining one. Then have a ball.

Another possibility—and perhaps the most comfortable way to commit adultery—is to swing. A great many people have no desire to destroy their marriages. But they seem to have a deep need to confirm their sexual attractiveness with a variety of partners. For them, swinging seems to be the answer. When played by the rules it provides the needed sexual diversion without the domestic risk. It is happily married adultery.

10. Hire divorce specialists. At the very first sign of trouble you must hire the best divorce attorney and the best divorce detective you can find. I have made no secret of my contempt for the average attorney, but I have the greatest respect for the handful of truly professional divorce lawyers I know. Your choice of an attorney can drastically alter the future of your life.

How do you find a good divorce attorney? Ask your friends who have gone through divorce. Ask your regular attorney. In my opinion the attorney should be a divorce specialist, not a general practitioner who dabbles in an occasional domestic squabble. Second (and I admit I am prejudiced), the good divorce attorney almost always works with a private detective. Today's laws are stacked in favor of the spouse who can prove sexual misconduct against the other. And the good attorney is not afraid to share his fee with a private detective who can compile the necessary evidence.

Good luck. If you faithfully follow these ten rules you are likely to enjoy many happy years of successful extramarital sex.

But remember, I may be watching you.